If we had told people we were going to build a new bug tracker, they would have told us we were completely nuts. A little research into the market would tell you that there are scores, maybe hundreds, of potential competitors, from mega-expensive corporate systems and free open source projects, to on-demand software-as-a-service applications and homegrown tools purpose built to do one thing and do it well. And then there's Microsoft Excel, the all-in-one list builder and charting tool, which is still incredibly popular among small software teams.

Had we considered the massive competition out there, we may have never created JIRA. Fortunately for us, we had some naïveté in our favour, and no one told us *not* to do it. We built JIRA to help us track our own consulting business, which is what Atlassian was in 2001, and in 2002 it became a full-fledged product.

There's two reasons JIRA was successful: an unexpected business model and its flexible architecture. In 2002, Atlassian's sales model was unlike any other business-to-business software tools. It wasn't free like an open source project, but it wasn't expensive either like products from big corporations. It didn't require any professional services to use. And there were no sales people. It caused some confusion in the market. *Can you help us set up an evaluation?* Um, just download it and try it. *How can we make changes to the license agreement?* You can't. It's one size fits all. *How much for a support agreement?* It's included. Free. *Can I send you a purchase order?* Sure, or you can use your credit card. *A credit card? To purchase enterprise software?*

Of course, JIRA's popularity is more than a price point and business model. Most of the developers who started working on JIRA in 2003 are still at Atlassian today, building atop one of the most feature-rich and flexible issue trackers available. Depending on which company is using it, JIRA has been called a bug tracker, issue tracker, defect tracker, task tracker, project management system, or help desk system. It's used by waterfall and agile development teams. It's used by some of the largest corporations in the world to help build their biggest products, and some people use it to manage their personal cross country moves. The permissions system has allowed JIRA to work for both private and public-facing projects.

An ecosystem has been built up around JIRA. As of the time of writing this foreword, there are 421 commercial and open source plugins to JIRA on the Atlassian Plugin Exchange, and hundreds of other integrations built by companies for in-house use or by vendors who sell complementary products. We're extremely excited for Matt's book, too. Matt has been a terrific partner who has built custom integrations for JIRA, extending it far and beyond. In some ways, this book is another plugin to JIRA, helping customers to squeeze more value from the application. It's sure to provide assistance to all the aforementioned customers—the big companies and the small ones, the ones looking to configure it as a bug tracker, and those looking for project management tool.

The final word is about our customers who have pushed the product, our product and support teams, and our imaginations, further then we could have ever done by ourselves. It's been a lot of fun, and for that, we say *thanks, mate*.

Mike Cannon-Brookes and Scott Farquhar, Atlassian co-founders and CEOs

Practical JIRA Administration
Using JIRA Effectively

Matthew B. Doar
with Mikey Schott

Beijing · Boston · Farnham · Sebastopol · Tokyo

Practical JIRA Administration

by Matthew B. Doar

Printed in the United States of America.

Published by O'Reilly Media, Inc., 1005 Gravenstein Highway North, Sebastopol, CA 95472.

O'Reilly books may be purchased for educational, business, or sales promotional use. Online editions are also available for most titles (*http://safaribooksonline.com*). For more information, contact our corporate/institutional sales department: 800-998-9938 or *corporate@oreilly.com*.

Editor: Mike Loukides	**Interior Designer:** David Futato
Production Editor: Kristen Borg	**Cover Designer:** Karen Montgomery
Proofreader: O'Reilly Production Services	**Illustrator:** Robert Romano

June 2011:   First Edition

Revision History for the First Edition

2011-05-23:   First Release
2012-02-29:   Second Release
2013-06-04:   Third Release
2015-10-01:   Fourth Release

See *http://oreilly.com/catalog/errata.csp?isbn=9781449305413* for release details.

978-1-449-30541-3

[LSI]

Table of Contents

Preface

What This Book Is About

This book is about *JIRA*, the popular issue tracker from *Atlassian*. An issue tracker lets people collaborate more effectively when there are things to be done. It also replaces copies of spreadsheets in email. You can use an issue tracker for everything from tracking bugs in software to customer support requests, and beyond. I like to say that JIRA is a big "To Do" list for teams.

The book is intended for readers who administer a JIRA instance or design how JIRA is used locally. It assumes a basic familiarity with what JIRA can do and provides more information about how JIRA is *intended* to be used.

Each chapter should help clarify some confusing aspect of JIRA administration. The chapters are only loosely connected to each other, with the intention that they can be read in any order. Most new administrators start with the chapters about schemes and workflows. Chapter 1 and Chapter 2 are "warm-up" chapters that deal with two specific aspects of JIRA administration. Chapter 3 through Chapter 5 covers more system-wide aspects such as schemes, workflows and making sure your changes don't affect other people unexpectedly. Chapter 7 through Chapter 11 covers upgrades, migrations and then finally some common frustrations with JIRA.

The intention of this book is to supplement but not repeat the extensive JIRA documentation, freely available at *http://confluence.atlassian.com/display/JIRA/JIRA+Documentation*.

In selecting the different topics to cover in this book, I was conscious of the different questions that I, as a software toolsmith, am asked about JIRA every day. I chose the most frequently asked and difficult ones. If you can't find a particular topic and think it should be in a book such as this, then please do contact me with more details.

Some of the topics that are covered are expanded versions of entries already posted to my old blog "Practical JIRA Development," at *http://jiradev.blogspot.com*. The chapters that are based on these entries are Chapter 1, Chapter 2, and Chapter 4.

JIRA Versions and System Details

The fourth release and current refers to version *7.0* which was released in October 2015. Where there are differences between versions of JIRA and the Atlassian-hosted JIRA Cloud service, these are noted in the text.

- The first release of this book referred to JIRA version *4.2.4 Standalone*, which was released in February 2011.
- The second release referred to version *5.0*, which was released in February 2012.
- The third release referred to version *6.0*, which was released in May 2013.

The target system used throughout this book is a Linux server with JDK 1.8 and MySQL. The main differences for other operating systems, deployment types, databases, and JVMs are the installation instructions and the names and paths of certain files. These details are described in the online JIRA documentation.

There are two main choices for deploying JIRA:

JIRA Server
> This is the original JIRA deployment package, also known as Standalone and Behind the Firewall (BTF). WAR packages for JIRA Server are no longer provided by Atlassian since JIRA 7.0.

JIRA Cloud
> Formerly known as Studio and OnDemand, this is the cloud version of JIRA. Some features of JIRA Server are not available in JIRA Cloud.

Development Environment

This book was written using OSX 10.10.4 on a MacBook Pro (Retina, mid-2014), using DocBook 4.5, Emacs 22.1.50.1 and git 1.7.5.4. The output files were generated using a custom web-based authoring tool named *Atlas*, developed by O'Reilly for their authors. Using a web-based tool allows books to be updated more frequently and the different output formats generated automatically.

Coauthor

The fourth update of this book for JIRA 7.0 includes a new chapter by my Service-Rocket colleague Mikey Schott (Chapter 6).

Mikey Schott
> Mikey has worked as a corrosion survey technician, a satellite janitor, and a record store employee, but seems to have found most success consulting and training people on JIRA. His non-paying gigs include community theater acting and crossword puzzle solver. He is also a member of the Atlassian Certification Advisory Board.

Technical Reviewers

Stafford Vaughan
> Stafford started using JIRA in 2005 after completing a Software Engineering degree in Australia and joining CustomWare, Atlassian's leading services partner. He is a founding author of Atlassian's official JIRA training course materials, and has spent the past five years delivering training to hundreds of organizations worldwide. Stafford currently lives in San Francisco and works in Silicon Valley at Apple.

Bryan Rollins
> Bryan is the General Manager for Atlassian JIRA.

Paul Slade
> Paul is a member of the Atlassian JIRA development team.

Matt Quail
> Matt is a member of the Atlassian JIRA development team.

Matt Silver
> Matt Silver has worked in the technical support field for 10 years and now works for Twitter. He's an avid rock drummer and lives in Northern California.

Roger Symonds
> Roger has built and run Atlassian training courses delivered globally to over 20,000 attendees, and personally delivered training at a hat-trick of Atlassian Summits. He's a Sydneysider who enjoys flying gliders and playing guitar.

Conventions Used in This Book

The following typographical conventions are used in this book:

Italic

> Indicates new terms, URLs, email addresses, filenames, and file extensions.

`Constant width`

> Used for program listings, as well as within paragraphs to refer to program elements such as variable or function names, databases, data types, environment variables, statements, and keywords.

`Constant width bold`

> Shows commands or other text that should be typed literally by the user.

`Constant width italic`

> Shows text that should be replaced with user-supplied values or by values determined by context.

Administration→System→System info

> Shows menu selections within JIRA, in this case the Administration menu item, the System menu item and then the System Info menu item. The Administration menu item is now a gear icon in the top right corner. Previous versions of JIRA had a separate menu item named "Administration." The shortcut *g g* is a helpful way to find specific administration action.

> This icon signifies a tip, suggestion, or general note.

> This icon indicates a warning or caution.

Using Code Examples

This book is here to help you get your job done. In general, you may use the code in this book in your programs and documentation. You do not need to contact us for permission unless you're reproducing a significant portion of the code. For example, writing a program that uses several chunks of code from this book does not require permission. Selling or distributing a CD-ROM of examples from O'Reilly books does require permission. Answering a question by citing this book and quoting example code does not require permission. Incorporating a significant amount of example code from this book into your product's documentation does require permission.

We appreciate, but do not require, attribution. An attribution usually includes the title, author, publisher, and ISBN. For example: *Practical JIRA Administration* by Matthew B. Doar with Mikey Schott (O'Reilly). Copyright 2015 Matthew B. Doar, 978-1-449-30541-3."

If you feel your use of code examples falls outside fair use or the permission given above, feel free to contact us at *permissions@oreilly.com*.

Safari® Books Online

 Safari Books Online is an on-demand digital library that lets you easily search over 7,500 technology and creative reference books and videos to find the answers you need quickly.

With a subscription, you can read any page and watch any video from our library online. Read books on your cell phone and mobile devices. Access new titles before they are available for print, and get exclusive access to manuscripts in development and post feedback for the authors. Copy and paste code samples, organize your favorites, download chapters, bookmark key sections, create notes, print out pages, and benefit from tons of other time-saving features.

O'Reilly Media has uploaded this book to the Safari Books Online service. To have full digital access to this book and others on similar topics from O'Reilly and other publishers, sign up for free at *http://safaribooksonline.com*.

How to Contact Us

Please address comments and questions concerning this book to the publisher:

O'Reilly Media, Inc.
1005 Gravenstein Highway North
Sebastopol, CA 95472
800-998-9938 (in the United States or Canada)
707-829-0515 (international or local)
707-829-0104 (fax)

We have a web page for this book, where we list errata, examples, and any additional information. You can access this page at:

http://oreil.ly/practicalJIRAadmin

To comment or ask technical questions about this book, send email to:

bookquestions@oreilly.com

For more information about our books, courses, conferences, and news, see our website at *http://www.oreilly.com.*

Find us on Facebook: *http://facebook.com/oreilly*

Follow us on Twitter: *http://twitter.com/oreillymedia*

Watch us on YouTube: *http://www.youtube.com/oreillymedia*

Content Updates

The complete list of changes in each release of JIRA can be found at *http://conflu ence.atlassian.com/display/JIRA/Production+Releases*. The End of Support announcements are located at *https://confluence.atlassian.com/display/JIRA/End+of+Support +Announcements+for+JIRA*. Reading the Release Notes and Upgrade Notes for each major release is particularly recommended. This section lists the changes that are related to this book.

February 29, 2012

The changes in JIRA 5.0 that are related to the content of this book include the following:

- The administration screens were all changed in JIRA 4.4.
- User directories were added to JIRA 4.3.
- The workflow graphic designer tool was shipped with JIRA 4.4.
- The REST API has been developed further, and as of JIRA 5.0, can now modify issues.
- JIRA now has Linux and Windows installers.

June 4th, 2013

The changes in JIRA 5.1, 5.2, and 6.0 that are related to the content of this book include the following:

- JIRA 5.2 and 6.x require Java 1.7.
- Usernames can be changed in JIRA 6.0.

- JIRA 6.0 updated the UI look and feel to match other Atlassian applications.
- JIRA 6.0 also introduced a new issue view in the Issue Navigator that shows more of each issue's details.
- Workflows and their associated fields and screens can be exported and imported more easily.
- Workflow schemes can be edited in place, without copying and updating every project that uses them.
- JIRA 6.0 displays better on mobile devices.
- Issue fields can now be edited without editing the whole issue.
- Users can be deactivated properly.
- Issue collectors can be defined for each project to make it easier for non-authenticated users to add content to JIRA.
- Links can be to issues in other JIRA instances and there is a JIRA to JIRA issue copy add-on.
- The website plugins.atlassian.com (PAC) was renamed to marketplace.atlassian.com, and the studio.plugins.atlassian.com website was removed.
- JIRA plugins were redefined as a specific type of *add-on*, and this release uses the term "add-on" in preference to "plugin." For more information, see *https://conflu ence.atlassian.com/display/JIRA/Managing+Add-ons*.

October 1st, 2015

The major changes in JIRA 6.1, 6.2, 6.3, 6.4, and 7.0 that are related to the content of this book include the following:

- JIRA 6.1 introduced the ability to change project keys as well as project names.
- The graphical workflow design was rewritten and its functionality extended.
- Project templates were added. These templates help you to use copies of standard workflows and screen schemes for particular kinds of work, e.g., an Agile team. JIRA 7.0 adds the ability to create a project using the schemes of an existing project ("Create with shared configuration").
- Integration between JIRA and other Atlassian products such as Stash and Bamboo has been increased. For example, you can create git branches for a bug from within JIRA.
- With the release of JIRA 7.0, SOAP access has finally been removed, along with the section about SOAP in Chapter 9 in previous releases.

- Custom icons for statuses were replaced by colored lozenges in JIRA 6.2. Project icons changed from squares to circles as part of the UI standardization of the Atlassian products.

- JIRA 6.1 introduced the Audit Log and 6.3 extended it. This allows JIRA administrators to track who changed the configuration of JIRA.

- JIRA 6.3 added a limited form of data import from CSV files for regular users.

- JIRA 6.3 introduced the concept of Data Center. Atlassian's Enterprise Data Center products allow multiple instances of JIRA to use the same database for improved performance for concurrent users, and better disaster recovery.

  Data Center is part of the Atlassian Enterprise Services program that includes Premier Support (PS) and Technical Account Managers (TAM). These offerings are intended for larger customers where JIRA is a critical business tool.

- JIRA 6.4 was released with Java 1.8, and JIRA 7.0 is not tested with Java 1.7. Along with other internal changes, this resulted in significant performance and stability improvements.

- JIRA 6.4 extended the idea of project templates and introduced a new project view that integrates JIRA Agile boards more closely with JIRA.

- In the JIRA Cloud environment, a new class of add-ons named Atlassian Connect has been developed. These add-ons use webhooks to send data to remote servers, then display the results in the JIRA Cloud instance. This model improves the stability of the JIRA server because nothing third-party is run directly in the same JVM as JIRA. It also helps solve the long-term issue that JIRA Cloud was not as customizable as JIRA Server.

 JIRA 7.0 introduced the idea of *applications*, which are related to how JIRA and the JIRA Agile and JIRA Service Desk add-ons are bundled. Three different logical packages now exist, each for a different kind of team:

- JIRA Core—the original JIRA application.
- JIRA Software—JIRA Core along with JIRA Agile. Intended for software development teams and others using Agile boards.
- JIRA Service Desk—JIRA Core plus the JIRA Service Desk add-on. For teams that work with help desks,

More detailed information about migrating to the JIRA 7 applications can be found at *https://confluence.atlassian.com/migration*.

Acknowledgments

People at Atlassian who have been particularly helpful over the years include Jonathan Nolen, Sarah Maddox (now Google), and Jessie Curtner. The Atlassian founders Mike Cannon-Brookes and Scott Farquhar, and all of the JIRA team have always been responsive and encouraging. The Atlassian Support teams have graciously put up with my detail-oriented comments and never-ending stream of issues, particularly Boris Berenberg and John Garcia. Thank you all!

Within the Atlassian community, Jamie Echlin, Nic Brough, Neal Applebaum, and Leonid Maslov stand out for the number of times they've answered questions from myself and others in the old JIRA Developer's Forum and its replacement site *Atlassian Answers*. Other experts that I have benefited from discussions with include Andy Brook, Jonathan Doklovic, David Fischer, Jobin Kuruvilla, Bob Swift, Vincent Thoulé, and David Vittor. Many thanks to all of you, and see you at the next Atlas Summit!

My sincere thanks also go to all the clients of Consulting Toolsmiths for directly and indirectly providing me with the knowledge of which parts of JIRA confuse many JIRA administrators. Many thanks to Rob Castaneda, Adam May, Jesse Miller, Yesi Cisneros and Mikey Schott and all my other colleagues at ServiceRocket (formerly CustomWare) for doing so many parts of a successful business that I'd rather not have to. More gong! (formerly cowbell)

Behind all I do is my dearest wife Katherine and beloved children Lizi, Jacob, and Luke. Thank you all, and may the love of God rest and remain with you always.

CHAPTER 1

Groups Versus Roles

Overview

The difference between JIRA groups and JIRA project roles seems to confuse many JIRA administrators. This chapter explains the differences and what each one is good for.

JIRA originally just had users and groups of users, and no project roles. Groups were pretty powerful—wherever you could do something with a user, you could generally use a group instead.

For instance, if you wanted to allow a specific user john.smith to change the Reporter field in a project's issues, you could:

1. Create a new permission scheme with a description something like "john.smith can change Reporter."

2. Next, add the john.smith user to the appropriate Modify Reporter permission entry in the new permission scheme.

3. Change the appropriate JIRA project to use the new permission scheme.

You could also do the same thing with a group:

1. Define a new JIRA group named "Can Modify Reporters."

2. Add the user john.smith to the new group.

3. Create a new permission scheme with a description something like "Added an extra group of users that can change Reporter."

4. Add the *group* (instead of the user) to the appropriate Modify Reporter permission entry in the new permission scheme.

5. Just as before, change the appropriate JIRA project to use the new permission scheme.

Both of these approaches now allow john.smith to change the Reporter field. So far so good, but there are two main problems with using JIRA groups like this: scaling and updating.

Scaling

If you want john.smith to be able to edit the Reporter field in some projects, and also allow a different user, jane.bloggs, to do the same thing in other projects, then you have to create two permission schemes, one for each user being granted this permission. If you then decide that they are both allowed to edit the Reporter in some shared projects, then you need a *third* permission scheme. With lots of users, this leads to an explosion in the number of permission schemes (and any other JIRA scheme that supports groups).

Keeping track of the difference between each of these permission schemes is tedious and error-prone, even with the scheme comparison tools (Administration→Scheme Tools), which are themselves deprecated in JIRA 6.4.

Updating

As time passes, users will likely need to be part of different JIRA groups. Only JIRA administrators can change the membership of JIRA groups. However project leads are allowed to make changes to project roles, and project leads usually know which project roles a user should currently be part of. Using project roles means fewer tasks for JIRA administrators.

Project Roles

What was needed to avoid these problems with JIRA groups was another level of indirection,[1] and that's exactly what JIRA project roles are. Figure 1-1 shows the basic idea.

---

1 "All problems in computer science can be solved by another level of indirection." — David Wheeler, the inventor of the subroutine.

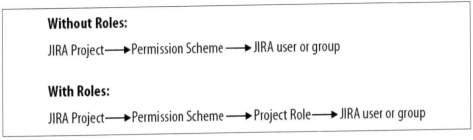

Without Roles:

JIRA Project ——▶ Permission Scheme ——▶ JIRA user or group

With Roles:

JIRA Project ——▶ Permission Scheme ——▶ Project Role ——▶ JIRA user or group

Figure 1-1. JIRA project roles

JIRA has three default project roles: *Administrators*, *Developers*, and *Users*. The current members of these roles for each project can be seen at Administration→Projects: click on the project name, then Roles.

The number and names of the roles can be changed at Administration→User management→Roles, but for now let's stick with the three default roles. Every JIRA project has the same set of project roles all the time. The default members of each role for new projects are shown in Figure 1-2. Note that the project lead is not a default member of the Administrators role and has to be explicitly added.

Project Role Name	Users	Groups
Administrators	None	jira-administrators
Developers	None	jira-developers
Users	None	jira-users

Figure 1-2. JIRA default roles and their memberships

For each role in every project, a JIRA administrator or a project administrator can define who plays that role by adding or removing a user or a group for the role.

For example, you could add an individual contractor using JIRA to the Users role for only the projects they need to work with. For such JIRA instances, I usually create a new JIRA group named something like "my-company-name-staff" and then replace the "jira-users" group with the new group throughout JIRA. I then create a JIRA group for each set of contractors and add that group to the appropriate project roles for select JIRA projects (and also to the "JIRA Users" permission at Administration→System→Global permissions).

Once you've chosen who plays each role for each project, you can use the roles in your schemes. For instance, when you look at the default permission scheme you'll see that all of the permissions are granted to project *roles*, not directly to users or groups. The significant thing about roles is that they can be changed *for each project* by people who are in the Administrators role but are not JIRA administrators. These people can now create versions and components for their project without needing to change the underlying configuration of JIRA or needing to be JIRA administrators.

To put all that another way:

Who can change a project's versions and components?
The users who have the Administer Projects permission.

Which users have the Administer Projects permission?
Check the specific permission scheme, but it's usually only people in the "Administrators" project role.

Which users have the Administrators project role?
Members of the *jira-administrators* group and anyone else that you add to that role for a project.

Who can change other parts of JIRA's configuration?
Only members of the *jira-administrators* group, not the users who have the Administrators project. Project administrators can't change workflows, for example.

Creating a New Project Role

Another way to understand what's going on here is to create a new project role. Let's say that for some reason, we want to allow the technical publications ("Tech Pubs") users assigned to each project to modify the Reporter of an issue.

The default permission scheme already allows users with an Administrator role in a project to modify the Reporter of an issue. But we don't want to allow the Tech Pubs user to administer the whole project: we just want to give them that one specific permission.

We can create a new role *Documentation*, at Administration→User management→Roles. We can also add our Tech Pubs lead bobby.jones as a default member in the "Users" column under "Manage Default Users" of the new project role so that he will be in the Documentation role for all new projects by default.

Now every JIRA project has this new role, since you can't add a new project role just for one JIRA project. When a new JIRA project is created, it will have the bobby.jones user in the Documentation role for the project. For existing projects, we can manually add the appropriate Tech Pubs user (or group) to the Documentation role for each project. Once the users for this role have been added, we can edit the appropriate permission schemes and add the Documentation role to the Modify Reporter permission entry. The permission scheme now checks which users are in the *role* for each project, rather than looking at a fixed list of users or groups of users.

If the Tech Pubs person changes for the project, then the people in the project role Administrator can change the members of the Documentation role for just that project. There is no need to ask a JIRA administrator to make the changes.

 An example of a good description for a newly created role is "This new project role is for identifying Facilities staff in non-Facilities projects." Creating a wiki page that describes the intended purpose of each new role is another good idea.

For more information about using project roles to control which users can view which projects, see "Hiding Projects from Users" on page 35.

From the other direction, you can also see which roles an individual user has in all the JIRA projects: go to Administration→User management→Users, find the user, and click on Project Roles.

The easiest way to allow everyone to see the members of each role for a JIRA project is to install the Project Role Tab add-on (*https://marketplace.atlassian.com/plugins/ jira.plugin.projectrole.projectroletab*). This add-on allows JIRA administrators to tell their users to contact the project administrators for certain changes.

Not Creating New Project Roles

Sometimes I see JIRA instances where roles have been treated like groups. This results in many roles being created, but many of these only make sense in a few projects. For instance, if you create a new role named Operations and then have a JIRA project for tracking job applications, there may be no obvious use for Operations and job applications. The best approach is to keep the number of roles as small and generic as possible. Some useful examples of names for extra roles are: Creators, Approvers, Managers, Workers, Testers and Schedulers. These names are generic and apply to more than just software development.

Another configuration problem I see is using user names in the default memberships of roles. What happens is that every new project has the user name set for the role, but when the user leaves, every project has to be modified to change the role. This is a good argument for using only groups as default role members.

One mistake I've seen have some serious consequences is using a project role in a notification scheme. This can happen when you want to allow project administrators to send specific users an email when an issue is created in their project. It's easy to create a project role such as *Notify on All Create Issue* and add it to the notification scheme. The problem is that a unknowing project administrator can add a large group such as *jira-users* to the project role and then every single person in *jira-users* will receive email when a new issue is created. In a large organization this can be thousands of users being spammed each time. I recommend not using project roles in notification schemes if possible.

 You should only create a new project role if you are going to use it in a scheme or workflow, and if it applies to all your JIRA projects.

Summary

JIRA groups are made up of JIRA users and can only be changed by JIRA administrators. But JIRA project roles are made up of JIRA users and JIRA groups and can be changed per project by project administrators. Project administrators are all the users in the Administrators role for a JIRA project.

 Should I use a group or a project role?

If you want to refer to the same set of more than about six users across multiple projects, use a group. Remember that group membership has to be maintained to be useful If you want to refer to a set of users that is potentially different per project, use a project role. Also, don't add new roles without considering whether the existing ones can be used in the permission scheme to accomplish what you are trying to do.

Further Reading

http://confluence.atlassian.com/display/JIRA/Managing+Groups discusses JIRA groups in general.

http://confluence.atlassian.com/display/JIRA/Managing+Project+Roles discusses JIRA Project Roles specifically.

Some of the background information to this chapter can be found at *https://conflu ence.atlassian.com/display/JIRA063/Migrating+User+Groups+to+Project+Roles*, along with the documentation for the JIRA Scheme Comparison Tools. Unfortunately, the scheme tools only work with Permission and Notification Schemes, and they are deprecated as of JIRA 6.4.

Holger Schimanski's Project Role Tab add-on (*https://marketplace.atlassian.com/ plugins/jira.plugin.projectrole.projectroletab*) is an good way to allow everyone to see who is in each role in a JIRA project. It currently costs nothing and the source code is freely available, though it is not a supported add-on.

CHAPTER 2

Resolved, Resolution, and Resolution Date

Overview

One thing that sometimes confuses both JIRA users and administrators is the difference between the Resolved status and the Resolution field. This chapter clears up some of the confusion between these very similar-sounding terms. The differences are summarized at the end of this chapter ("Summary" on page 11).

Getting this right is important, because many of the standard JIRA reporting gadgets on dashboards expect the Resolution field to be set as expected—otherwise confusing results occur. For example, gadgets that refer to the date when issues were resolved use the Resolution Date field, which is in turn based on the Resolution field.

Resolved

JIRA comes with a default workflow (Administration→Issues→Workflows) named "jira," shown later in Figure 5-1 and summarized below in Figure 2-1. This workflow has the following statuses for an issue, shown in the order they commonly occur.

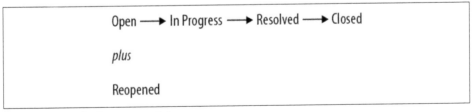

Figure 2-1. Default JIRA workflow

The idea is that an issue (such as a bug) is created with a status of *Open*, and is then moved to *In Progress* and then *Resolved* by the person who fixes it. The bug is then moved to either *Closed* or *Reopened* by someone who checks whether it really was fixed or not. So "Resolved" is just a name for an issue status. The status could just as well have been named "Believed Fixed" or "Ready for Testing."

If you create a workflow from scratch (see Chapter 5), the Resolved status is not connected in any way with the Resolution field.

Resolution

It's generally a good idea to keep the number of statuses in your workflow as small as possible to make maintenance easier. It makes sense to avoid having lots of statuses with names like:

"Closed and Fixed"
"Closed and Won't Fix"
"Closed Because It's A Duplicate"
"Closed Since…"

The Resolution system field (Administration→Issues→Resolutions) can be used to avoid having lots of similar statuses. The default values for Resolution of Fixed, Won't Fix, Duplicate, Incomplete, Cannot Reproduce, Done and Won't Do cover many of the ways that an issue could be closed, and you can change this list if necessary. I find that a Complete resolution is often useful for generic tasks that are finished. Canceled is a gentler form of Won't Fix, but has spelling variants. Once the Resolution field in an issue contains any value at all, then links to that issue will have a line through them to indicate that the issue is resolved.

The intended use of the Resolution field is that when a bug is created, the field is empty, with *no value at all*. This is displayed in an issue as a value of "Unresolved." When an issue is moved to a status such as Resolved or Closed, the Resolve Issue Screen is usually shown during the transition. This screen includes the Resolution field, ready for the user to set a value. A bug can have its Resolution set to "Fixed" while it is moving to the Resolved status, for example.

JIRA expects the Resolution field to be set in any status you would consider an issue resolved, and that the Resolution field should be cleared in all other statuses. It's up to you to make sure this happens, with a transition screen or post function when you create or modify workflows (see Chapter 5).

In the default JIRA workflow, the Resolve Issue Screen is the only screen where you can set the Resolution field for an issue, and this screen is only used for transitions to the Resolved and Closed statuses. In your own workflows you are responsible for making sure that the Resolution is set. Once the Resolution has been set, the issue is considered *resolved* by JIRA, even if the status of the issue is not the Resolved status but some other status defined by you (such as "Deployed").

 The only way to remove the resolution from an issue in a standard JIRA installation is to *Reopen* an issue. Adding the Resolution field to the Default Screen or any other non-transition screen to make it easier to change is a bad idea, because it is a required field and will get set for issues that aren't yet resolved. You can see which screens the Resolution field is on by looking at any field configuration (Administration→Issues→Field configurations)

Another approach for cleaning up the results of an incorrect workflow and clearing the Resolution field in an issue is to create transitions back to the same status that have a post function to clear the Resolution. The ability to create transitions back to the same status is a non-obvious and useful ability for workflow designs.

One way to make sure you don't have problems with the Resolution field and custom workflows is to create and save the JQL filter: status = Open and resolution is not empty order by created desc. This filter should always return zero issues. If there are Open issues with a resolution set being created, then you can look at a recent issue's History tab and see where the resolution was not cleared. You can even set up a filter subscription to email any non-zero results to you.

A similarly useful query is status = Closed and resolution is empty order by created desc, which helps find workflows where the Close transition does not set the Resolution field. This filter should also return zero issues.

Resolution Date

The Resolution Date system field is the latest date that *any* value was set in the Resolution system field for that issue. The Resolution Date field will only be empty if there is no value at all in the Resolution field.

 The Resolution Date is confusingly named *Resolved* in the list of Issue Navigator columns and some gadgets. This has nothing directly to do with the status named "Resolved."

Other Approaches

Some organizations using JIRA don't use the Resolution field for a number of reasons:

- It's hard to reset the value to empty for unresolved issues.
- The resolution field doesn't appear on standard screens, only during transitions.
- If the Resolution field is used on any custom transition screens, it's hard to make the field not be required.

Instead, they base their reporting only on the name of the statuses in the workflows. They may also create their own custom Select List field named something like *Our Resolution* or *Sub-status*, with its own values such as Unresolved, Fixed, Won't Fix, Duplicate, Incomplete, and Cannot Reproduce.

The drawback of not using the system Resolution field as JIRA intended is that many of the standard JIRA gadgets are no longer useful. Making sure that the Resolution is set correctly in your workflow is a better approach in the long run (see the section "Implementing a Workflow" on page 49).

The options for the Resolution field are defined for all JIRA projects and workflows. Sometimes you may want to restrict the resolutions used in a workflow. One way to do this is to use *Workflow Properties*. Another way to do this per issue type is to have a custom field with the Resolution options you want for each issue type, and then use a workflow post function to set the Resolution system field based on the value of the custom field (thanks to Joanna Thurmann for that idea).

A helpful approach to consider in custom workflows is creating a transition for each desired resolution, with a post function in each transition to set the resolution *without* using a screen. For example, there could be a transition from the current status to Closed named "Duplicate," which *automatically* sets the resolution to Duplicate.

Adding a resolution named "Unresolved" to the system Resolution field is a bad idea, because since the Resolution field now has a value, the issue will still be treated as resolved by the standard JIRA gadgets.

Summary

- "Resolved" is just the name of one of the issue statuses in the default JIRA workflow.
- Resolution is a system field with values of Fixed, Not Fixed, and so on. The Resolution field is only set during transitions.
- Don't add the Resolution field to any screen except a transition screen.
- An unresolved issue is one with *no value* in the Resolution field.
- A resolved issue is one with *any value* in the Resolution field. Links to a resolved issue have a line through their displayed URL.
- The Resolution Date system field is the latest date that the Resolution field was changed to any value.

Further Reading

Some of the points in this chapter are mentioned briefly at *https://confluence.atlassian.com/display/JIRA/Configuring+Workflow#ConfiguringWorkflow-OpenandClosedissuesdefined* and in the comments there.

Clearing the Resolution field is covered at *https://confluence.atlassian.com/display/JIRAKB/How+to+clear+the+resolution+field+when+the+issue+is+reopened*.

The problem of the Resolution Date changing when an issue's status is updated was described in the JIRA bug *JRA-20286* and fixed in JIRA 4.3.1.

The *Created vs Resolved Gadget* described at *http://confluence.atlassian.com/display/JIRA/Adding+the+Created+vs+Resolved+Gadget* is a good example of where confusion can occur about what "Resolved" actually means—it's the Resolution field, not the Resolved status.

CHAPTER 3

Understanding Schemes

Overview

Schemes are a major part of configuring JIRA, but they are also one of the most confusing parts of JIRA. This chapter is intended to clear up some of that confusion. Chapter 4 has a worked example of how schemes can be used to configure JIRA.

A JIRA *scheme* is a collection of configured values that can be used by one or more JIRA projects. For example, a Notification scheme describes who receives email when issues are changed. The same Notification scheme can be used by more than one JIRA project. In fact, the Default Notification scheme is used by all JIRA projects unless you configure a project differently.

The seven schemes that are active for a particular JIRA project can be viewed and edited by editing the project (go to Administration→Projects and click on the project name, not Edit).

We'll cover the four schemes that are similar to the Notification scheme first and look at the remaining three (more complex) schemes later. The top-level page in the Atlassian documentation for all of this information is *http://confluence.atlassian.com/display/JIRA/Defining+a+Project*.

Project-Wide Schemes

The four schemes like the Notification scheme that apply either to the whole JIRA project, or to *all* issue types within a project are:

Issue Type Scheme
What issue types (Bug, New Feature etc) can be used in a particular JIRA project

Notification Scheme
> Who receives what email when an issue changes

Permission Scheme
> Who can do what to an issue

Issue Security Scheme
> Who can even view an issue

First we'll take a quick detour to see how JIRA refers to users in such schemes.

Adding Users to Schemes

There are a dozen different ways (shown in Figure 3-1) that JIRA lets you specify a set of users, but happily the same ways can be used in both Notification and Permission Schemes. Issue Security schemes use a subset of these choices.

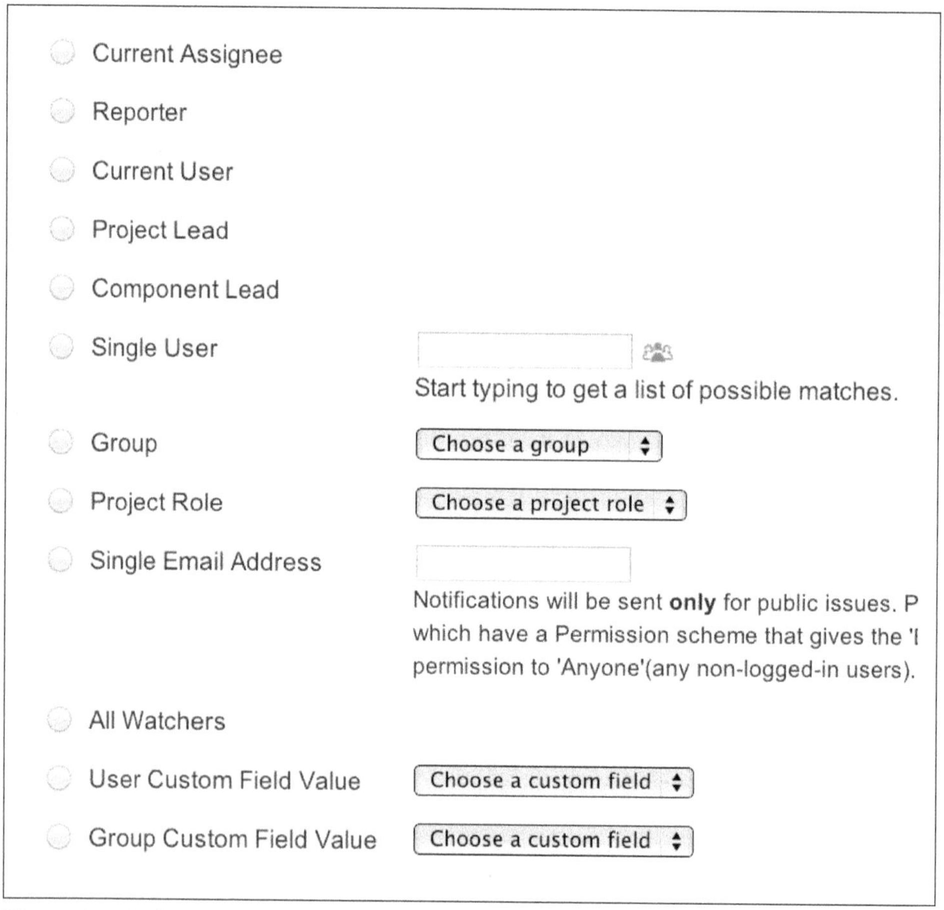

Figure 3-1. Referring to users in a scheme

The simplest of these are:

Current Assignee
The user that the issue is currently assigned to.

Reporter
The reporter of the issue; usually the JIRA user who originally created the issue.

Current User
For permission schemes, the user who is logged in.

Project Lead

Component Lead
The project lead is specified in each project's settings. Component leads are optionally configured for each component in a project.

Single Email Address
A specific email address. This only works for issues that can be browsed anonymously. Before JIRA 5 the email is formatted as text, not HTML.

All Watchers
All users listed in the system field Watchers for an issue.

The not-so-obvious ways are:

Single User
A username such as `john.smith`, *not* their full name such as "John Q. Smith."

Group

Project Role
A JIRA group of users or a JIRA project role. In general, use a Project Role instead of a Group, as discussed in Chapter 1.

User Custom Field Value
Use the contents of a custom field of type User Picker or Multi User Picker. Such a field might be populated during a transition or by editing an issue.

Group Custom Field Value
Use the contents of a custom field of type Group Picker or Multi Group Picker. In a notification scheme, all the members of these groups will receive email, so be careful about how many users are involved.

Issue Type Schemes

A JIRA project's issue type scheme controls which issue types are available for use in that project, as shown in Figure 3-2. For instance, most JIRA projects that are not used by developers should not have the Bug issue type shown as a choice anywhere.

You can define an issue type scheme by going to Administration→Issues→Issue types and clicking on *Issue type schemes*. You can also set the default issue type that will be used when someone is creating an issue, and even change the order of issue types that the user will see.

 Don't use the Default Issue Type Scheme in your JIRA projects. Every new issue type that is created gets added to that scheme. So over time people using a project will see a wider and confusing choice of issue types to use. You should define an issue type scheme with a specific set of issue types and use that instead.

Changing any scheme for lots of projects is generally a long and repetitive task (see "Managing Projects" on page 118), but not for issue type schemes. The *Associate* link in the list of issue type schemes allows you to select multiple projects to change at once.

For more information, see the documentation at *https://confluence.atlassian.com/display/JIRA/Associating+Field+Behavior+with+Issue+Types*.

Issue Type Scheme:
A subset of issue types

Figure 3-2. Issue Type Scheme

Notification Schemes

A notification scheme controls who receives what email about changes to JIRA issues. The default notification scheme sends emails to the reporter, assignee and watchers of an issue. Email messages are sent out from JIRA at most once per minute, and have to be sent to each individual user in turn to make sure that the permission scheme and issue security scheme are respected. So if a user doesn't have permission to view an issue, they won't receive email when the issue is changed.

It's much easier to add changes to a notification scheme than to undo them. So always keep an unchanged copy of the default notification scheme as an easy way to undo any changes you make later on. The first copy of a default scheme is often named something like "My Company Default Notification Scheme." I sometimes add a prefix "DO NOT USE" to the name of the default notification and permission schemes to make it obvious when the default schemes are still being used by a project.

JIRA uses an *event-driven* model for its notifications. When something such as a comment or a status change happens to a JIRA issue, a specific kind of *Event* is sent within JIRA. Another part of JIRA listens for events and acts on them when they are received. For example, when the JIRA system Mail Listener (Administration→System→Listeners) receives an event from an issue, it uses the notification scheme for the issue's project to decide who should receive the email. This process is summarized in Figure 3-3. The actual set of users who are sent email for each different event can be defined in the various ways listed in "Adding Users to Schemes" on page 14.

Notification Scheme:

An issue's status changes and a workflow post-function sends an event
  or
An issue changes and this sends an event

A Mail listener receives the event and looks up the notification scheme for the issue's project

The type of the event controls which users are sent email

Figure 3-3. Notification Scheme

You can define your own custom events at Administration→System→Advanced→ Events, and then change the post function in a workflow transition to make it send ("fire") the new event. The new event will appear as a new row in all the notification schemes, and you can then define who should receive email when that transition takes place.

Note that you cannot configure the type of event sent for non-workflow issue operations such as Assign or Comment.

It's important to avoid spamming your users with too much email, or they'll just filter it and miss useful information. Be careful how many users you add to a notification scheme. You can also share an issue or list of issues via email directly using the *Share* button or by typing @userid to send email to the user userid.

For more information, see the documentation at *http://confluence.atlassian.com/display/JIRA/Creating+a+Notification+Scheme*.

Permission Schemes

A permission scheme is how you configure who is allowed to do what to a JIRA issue. There are a number of fine-grained permissions, such as "Create Issues" and "Edit Issues." Each of these permissions has a set of users that are granted that permission, as shown in Figure 3-4. Just like notification schemes, this set of users can be configured in the various ways described in "Adding Users to Schemes" on page 14.

Permission Scheme:

Permission A: one set of users
Permission B: another set of users

Figure 3-4. Permission Scheme

Just like other schemes, it's much easier to make changes to a permission scheme than to undo them. Keep an unchanged copy of the default permission scheme as an easy way to undo any changes you make later on, or rename the default permission scheme with a prefix of "DO NOT USE."

Once defined, such permissions are used by JIRA in various ways. The most obvious permissions do what they say (e.g., "Link Issues" controls whether a user can link one issue to another). Other permissions such as Transition Issue, Edit Issue, Resolve Issue and Close Issue can be used in workflow conditions to control who can change an issue's status.

However, some of the permissions have effects that are not as obvious at first glance. For instance, when editing an issue, the Resolve Issue permission is needed to see the Fix Versions field, and the Schedule Issues permission is needed to see the Due Date field. If the user does not have those permissions, then these fields are hidden—not just grayed out—in an issue's edit screen.

As a guideline when creating a new permission scheme, use project roles rather than groups for each permission. This makes the permission scheme useful in more projects. Administrators can usually be given all of the available permissions. To stop users viewing the project and all its issues, use the Browse Projects permission.

When you give a User Custom Field Value or Group Custom Field Value a permission, if the field is empty it behaves exactly like the Anyone permission. For example if you grant Edit permission to members of a Multi User Picker field, then when the field is empty that means anyone. I would expect that an empty field would mean no-one could edit the issue, but that is not the case (see JRA-26659).

For more information, see the documentation at *http://confluence.atlassian.com/display/JIRA/Managing+Project+Permissions*.

Issue Security Schemes

An issue security scheme controls who can view or edit a *specific issue*. In practice, most JIRA projects don't need to have an Issue Security scheme defined, which is why this scheme is set to "None" by default when you create a new project.

Within an issue security scheme, you can define one or more "security levels" as shown in Figure 3-5. There is actually no hierarchy involved in these levels; they're really just sets of users. Each security level can have users assigned to it in the same way that was described in "Adding Users to Schemes" on page 14. You can also choose one level to be a default security level for the scheme. Users can belong to more than one security level and will see issues that are in any of their levels as you would expect.

Issue Security Scheme:

Security level A: one set of users
Security level B: another set of users

Figure 3-5. Issue Security Scheme

There is a system field in all issues named "Security Level," which contains a list of all the different levels configured in the issue security scheme that are active for that issue's project. Once a security level has been set in this field in an issue, then only users in that level can view or edit the issue. For other users, the issue is invisible and doesn't appear in searches, or recent issue lists either. If you have permission to change the security level of an issue you won't be allowed to change to a level you're not in, so that you don't create issues and then accidentally make them invisible to yourself.

To be able to set the Issue Security field in an issue to anything but the default value, you need to have the Set Issue Security permission ("Permission Schemes" on page 18). The default permission scheme does not give any user this permission. The project role Administrators is generally a good choice.

As an example of using an issue security scheme, if you are using JIRA as a help desk for external customers you can use an issue security scheme that only allows the Reporter and your staff to see each issue. That way, confidential information in a support request from one customer was not seen by another customer. JIRA Service Desk (*https://www.atlassian.com/software/jira/service-desk*) is a JIRA add-on from Atlassian that helps you configure JIRA for this use case, along with lots of other features.

For more information on issue security schemes, please see the documentation at *https://confluence.atlassian.com/display/JIRA/Configuring+Issue-level+Security*.

Schemes That Use Issue Types

Every JIRA project has three other schemes whose behavior depends upon the issue type of an issue. For example, the fields for a Bug may be quite different from the fields for a Task—this is defined in a field configuration scheme.

These schemes are more complex than schemes that don't depend on the issue type, so they're the schemes that usually confuse JIRA administrators. One way to keep the two kinds of schemes separate is to remember that only workflows, fields, and screens can depend on issue types.

The three schemes that use an issue's issue type are:

Workflow Scheme
    Which workflow is used for each issue type

Field Configuration Scheme
    Which fields are part of each issue type

Issue Type Screen Scheme
    Where the fields are displayed in an issue's screen

All of these schemes have the concept of a default. This is what is used if an issue type is not specifically mentioned in the scheme.

Different JIRA projects can all have totally different schemes, but to make maintenance easier you should always try to define schemes that can be reused by more than one project. This is discussed in "Working with Schemes" on page 25, where defining schemes for a project category is suggested.

Workflow Schemes

JIRA is designed to support different workflows. A workflow is a set of statuses and the transitions between them. A workflow *scheme* defines which workflow is used for each issue type, as shown in Figure 3-6. A default workflow can also be chosen in a workflow scheme, and this workflow will be used for all issue types that aren't specifically mentioned in the scheme.

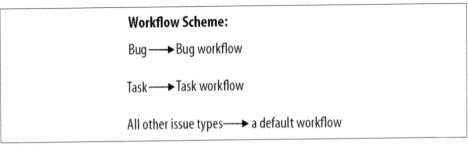

Figure 3-6. Workflow scheme

 The workflow scheme is an example of a common naming pattern for these three JIRA schemes: the Workflow *Scheme* is the mapping from an issue type to a *Workflow*. Similarly, the Field Configuration *Scheme* is the mapping from an issue type to a *Field Configuration*. However, the Issue Type Screen Scheme is a mapping from an issue type to a *Screen Scheme*.

One common practice is to start with a single workflow for the default and to then add workflows for specific issue types as necessary. For example, begin with a custom "My Company Default Workflow," then add a "Bug Workflow," a "Task Workflow," and so on. This is covered in more detail in Chapter 5.

For more information about Workflow Schemes, please see the documentation at *http://confluence.atlassian.com/display/JIRA/Activating+Workflow*.

Field Configuration Schemes

A field configuration scheme defines which Field Configuration is used for each issue type, as shown in Figure 3-7. A default field configuration can also be set.

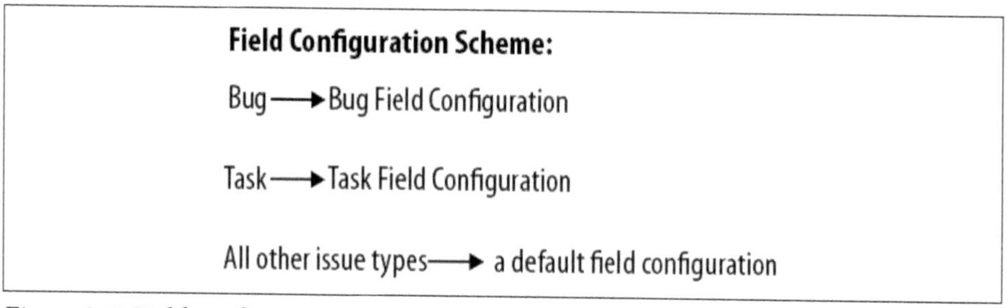

Field Configuration Scheme:

Bug ⟶ Bug Field Configuration

Task ⟶ Task Field Configuration

All other issue types ⟶ a default field configuration

Figure 3-7. Field configuration scheme

A *Field Configuration* (which is not a scheme) is a list of all the possible fields in any issue, with further configuration so that each field is valid and therefore "shown," or invalid and "hidden." For instance, the Fix Versions field is useful for a Bug but maybe not for a Task, so it could be configured as hidden in the Task Field Configuration.

When you edit a field configuration, you'll notice that every possible field is listed, whether or not the field is restricted by issue type or project. This is the expected behavior.

Each field can also be marked as "Required," which means that it can't be left empty. JIRA will try to not allow you to make a field both required and hidden. If you make a field required, also check that it appears on the screens used for creating and editing an issue. The next time the issue with a new required field is edited, the field will be required before the changes can be saved.

You can change a field's description in a field configuration, and also change the way that the contents of the field are displayed using various renderers. The renderers can show the contents of a field as raw text or can treat the text as wiki markup. If your users complain about JIRA mangling characters in the description or that they can't use wiki markup such as *{noformat}*, check which renderer is being used. The wiki renderer is the default renderer for the system fields Description, Environment, and Comments.

A field's description is also a convenient place to add JavaScript to tweak the behavior of a field. One example of this is shown in this jiradev blog post (*http://jiradev.blog spot.com/2011/12/prepopulating-jira-system-fields.html*), though maintaining such JavaScript after JIRA upgrades can become a lot of work and is not recommended. A better approach is to use the Behaviours part of the *ScriptRunner* add-on.

For more information about Field Configuration Schemes, see the documentation at *https://confluence.atlassian.com/display/JIRA/Associating+Field+Behavior+with +Issue+Types*.

Issue Type Screen Schemes (ITSS)

A screen in JIRA is just a column of fields. The fields may be system fields such as Summary and Description or custom fields. JIRA does not allow you to use a grid of fields on a screen.

I've saved the most complex and confusing scheme for last. All the other JIRA schemes either control the behavior of an entire JIRA project (issue type, permission, notification, issue security schemes) or control the behavior per issue type. An Issue Type Screen Scheme (ITSS) controls how the fields are displayed for an issue, that is, which order the fields should appear on the screen.

An ITSS uses *two* levels of indirection instead of just one. This is shown in Figure 3-8 and Figure 3-9.

 Other things to note about this scheme are that an "Issue Type *Screen* Scheme" is entirely different from a "Issue Type Scheme," and also that the phrase "Screen Scheme" is a great tongue-twister. Try it!

Recall that a field configuration scheme and its field configurations define the fields that are valid for a particular project and issue type. A field can be shown in a field configuration, but if it doesn't appear on any screens, the only place you'll see the field is when it is listed as a column to display in the Issue Navigator. Basically, screens control how these fields are *viewed* by a user.

On the first level of indirection we have Screen Schemes, which are not used directly by a JIRA project. Each Screen Scheme refers to up to three screens—one for creating an issue, one for viewing an issue, and one for editing an issue. This is so that you can have the same set of fields displayed in a different order on each screen, or not show certain fields during issue creation if they don't make sense there.

I often define a screen scheme for a single issue type. For example, you might have a Bug Screen Scheme that defines how to display the fields for a Bug during creation, viewing, and editing an issue, as shown in Figure 3-8.

At the second level of indirection, an ITSS defines which screen scheme should be used for each issue type. A default screen scheme can also be chosen in an ITSS.

To summarize, an ITSS tells JIRA which screen scheme should be used for a particular issue type in a project. Then a screen scheme tells JIRA which screen should be used for creating, viewing, or editing an issue.

For more information, see the online documentation at *https://confluence.atlassian.com/display/JIRA/Associating+Field+Behavior+with+Issue+Types*.

Bug Screen Scheme:

Default ⟶ Bug Screen

or for a more complex screen scheme:

Bug Screen Scheme:

Create ⟶ Bug Create Screen

View ⟶ Bug View Screen

Edit ⟶ Bug Edit Screen

Figure 3-8. Screen scheme

Issue Type Screen Scheme:

Bug ⟶ Bug Screen Scheme
Task ⟶ Task Screen Scheme
All other issue types ⟶ A default screen scheme

Bug Screen Scheme:

Create ⟶ Bug Create Screen
View ⟶ Bug View Screen
Edit ⟶ Bug Edit Screen

Task Screen Scheme:

Create ⟶ Task Create Screen
View ⟶ Task View Screen
Edit ⟶ Task Edit Screen

Default Screen Scheme:

Create ⟶ Default Create Screen
View ⟶ Default View Screen
Edit ⟶ Default Edit Screen

Figure 3-9. Issue Type Screen Scheme

Working with Schemes

Even once you understand what the seven different schemes do in JIRA, they will still need to be maintained. Every time that someone asks you to add a new field just for them, you will want to consider the effects of that change on everyone else's issues. Chapter 4 looks at how to make sure this happens in a controlled way, and the rest of this chapter covers some of the details of making this possible.

There is a necessary balance between the number of schemes and what they all do. I try to have only as many schemes as are needed by the different communities using a particular JIRA instance. You can configure JIRA so that every project has a complete set of schemes, but that could make for a lot of maintenance work later on. Also, if every group in an organization has a different process then working together is going to be that much harder.

 The most important thing to do before changing schemes is to *create a backup of your JIRA data*. If possible, test all scheme changes on a development or staging JIRA server. Even better, do both. All JIRA licenses can be used in one production and one development instance. You can also download a Developer license for this purpose from *https://my.atlassian.com* under your main license.

Choosing Schemes

Rather than allowing users to request many small changes to the schemes for their JIRA project, a better approach is define a set of predefined schemes and ask them to choose one from each. This "supermarket" approach also makes it easier for users to describe what they need as a change from something more commonly used.

For instance, some common workflows that users can choose from might be defined as:

Standard Simple Workflow
    Open, In Progress, Closed

Standard Testing Workflow
    Open, In Progress, Ready for Testing, Closed

Standard Approval Workflow
    Open, Approved, In Progress, Closed

Standard Approval and Testing Workflow
    Open, Approved, In Progress, Ready for Testing, Closed

Documenting Schemes

Each scheme has a name and an optional description. What are good names for schemes? Obviously it's a personal preference, but I usually name my schemes using a Project Category or Issue Type name, and then the scheme type.

For example, I might have a project category named "Customer Support" for all of the Customer Support department's JIRA projects. For an ITSS used by all those projects, I would use a name such as "Customer Support ITSS"—and then this scheme would refer to screen schemes with names like "Support Request Screen scheme" and "Training Screen scheme," using the issue type name as part of each screen scheme name.

I occasionally use the scheme's description field to record the latest change at the beginning, just after the summary of what a screen is for. The maximum length of the description varies according to the underlying database, but you can assume at least 4000 characters.

Sometimes I also add version numbers to a scheme's description or name, and update these when I change the scheme. This is useful, but I recommend adding the date as well, since you may end up with branched schemes. Workflows record the date and user who last changed them in their XML definition, and changes to other schemes appear in the Audit Log at Administration→System→Audit Log.

If the JIRA configuration is particularly complicated, then I may create a document describing the intended purpose of each scheme and the changes that have been made to it over time. This helps me when I'm trying to work out the effects of a proposed change to a particular scheme. I also add JIRA issue keys to scheme descriptions, where the issue contains the request for the change to the scheme.

Debugging Schemes

Sometimes you have to try to understand how a JIRA instance has been configured by another person whose documentation and naming of schemes was perhaps minimal. This usually happens when someone asks you something like "why can't I edit this field anymore?"

This type of task has become easier since JIRA 5.2, thanks to three new features for administrators in the bundled JIRA Admin Helper add-on. When creating or editing an issue, there is a link under the *Configure Fields* menu to "Where is my field?". This lets you specify a field by name, and then the various schemes are checked to see what is affecting that field. The other two features are the *Permission Helper* and *Notification Helper*, which help debug why a user does not have a certain permission or is not receiving notifications. These helpers are both available from the *Admin* button when viewing an issue. These helpers are the best place to start when debugging problems.

If you're not using the helpers, then the first thing to do is to see if the names of the various schemes bear any resemblance to what they are actually used for. Just because a scheme is called "Bug Workflow scheme" doesn't mean that it's only (or even) being used for bugs. The fastest way to get this information is to go to each scheme administration page and look at the projects that each scheme is assigned to. With luck, you'll spot an obvious pattern. If the scheme names don't end in "scheme," consider adding that to make it clear that it's a workflow *scheme*, not a workflow (for example).

You may also want to compare two schemes to see how they differ. Up until JIRA 6.3 there is a tool for comparing permission and notification schemes available at Administration→System→Scheme Tools. For other scheme types, I find that opening each scheme in a separate tab in my browser allows me to compare them reasonably well side-by-side.

If you decide to do a wholesale renaming of the schemes in your JIRA instance, then I recommend making a backup (of course) and then renaming just one collection of similar projects at a time (such as those with the same project category). Renaming old scheme names with an obvious prefix such as "OLD" can also help you spot the cases that you've missed. Since you've got a backup, you can also consider deleting inactive schemes.

Once you have a better understanding of which schemes exist and what they're used for, you can debug the original problem. My process for debugging most scheme problems is as follows:

1. Obtain a specific issue key where the problem can be reproduced.
2. If you can, get a sense of when the problem began, since it may be related to some other scheme change you've just made.
3. Note the project, issue type, and status of the issue, and also whether the problem occurs during creating, viewing, or editing the issue.
4. Go to Administration→Projects and click on the project name.
5. Note the names of the seven schemes that are currently being used by this project.
6. For each scheme in turn, view the details of the individual scheme and see what applies for the specific issue type. Note this information down as well.
7. If the problem is about a field, then view the appropriate field configuration and the create, edit, or view screen. The field may be hidden, required, not present on the screen, or present but in another screen tab.

   A custom field may also be restricted in the custom field context (Administration→Issues→Custom fields) to only certain issue types or projects.

Some fields are only visible if the user has the correct permission, so an administrator may not have the same problem as a user. Try creating a user account with the same groups and project roles as the user reporting the problem. Alternatively, log in as the user who reported the problem using either the *SU for JIRA* or the *ScriptRunner* add-ons.

8. If the problem is about a workflow action, check the specific transition's conditions and validators first.

9. If the problem seems related to some other scheme, then drill down into that scheme's definition, bearing in mind the issue type and where the problem was seen.

10. Once you have identified the root cause and fixed it, revert the fix and confirm that the same problem reappears, then fix it again. This confirms that your analysis and changes are correct. You should also check other schemes where the same problem may also exist.

Don't make any change to schemes before making a backup. Ideally, you should debug and fix the problem in a development instance of JIRA before touching the production JIRA.

The Future of Schemes

Schemes have always been a powerful and potentially confusing part of JIRA. JIRA versions since 4.4 contain much improved project administration screens that show more information in one place about how each JIRA project is configured. The underlying way that schemes work hasn't changed since before JIRA 4.0, however.

With the release of JIRA 6.4, there is an increased emphasis on using project templates. A project template allows you to choose a project type for a JIRA project on creation such as *SCRUM Agile*, and JIRA creates copies of some standard template schemes for the new project. This leads to each JIRA project having its own seven schemes which makes it easier to change one project and not accidentally affect any other projects. However it does mean that there will be many more schemes for administrators to manage: possibly seven for each project. For large JIRA instances I recommend choosing the Classic JIRA project which allows you to set the specific schemes.

As an aside, he new "Where is my field?" features are also typical of how Atlassian makes medium-to-large feature changes to JIRA. First an add-on is developed that offers the functionality in parallel to the existing functionality, but in a harmless way. Feedback and fixes occur rapidly and then the add-on (`jira-admin-helper-plugin`) is bundled with the shipped JIRA package (5.2 in this case). Many of the core features of JIRA are in fact add-ons when you look at their source code. Such add-ons can be disabled at Administration→Add-ons, System, but you should test carefully before doing this in production.

CHAPTER 4

JIRA as a Platform

Overview

A common request that JIRA administrators receive is to use JIRA for more than its current purpose. The typical case is that someone in one group tells a different group that "you can do that with JIRA, and it's already installed." After all, a JIRA project is like a spreadsheet with a line for each JIRA issue and a column for each field. It's true that JIRA can be used to track many different kinds of issues, and Chapter 3 described how to configure JIRA schemes to do just that.

This idea is, in effect, using JIRA as a *platform* for different web applications or "vertical solutions" for each group of users. There might be one such web application for Engineering JIRA projects, one for Customer Support JIRA projects, and so on. Using JIRA as a platform in this way is part of how it is designed to be used, but it does need a consistent configuration approach to be successful. This is particularly true if different groups don't want to see any part of other groups in the same JIRA instance.

However there isn't much documentation on how to do this in a *consistent* manner. This chapter describes one way to do this using a worked example, and then summarizes this in the section "Summary" on page 41.

What Can Be Configured

For each pair of a JIRA project and issue type, we can change the following:

- Which system and custom fields an issue can use, and whether they are required or not
- The order in which custom fields appear on an issue screen
- The workflow for an issue, including the statuses available in an issue

On a per-project basis, we can also configure:

- The issue types used in the project
- The components and versions available for an issue
- The permissions for what a user can do with an issue, including even knowing the issue exists
- Who can access the whole project
- Who receives email about changes to issues

What Is Configured System-Wide

Some configurations for JIRA are system-wide and affect all the users of a JIRA instance. Such configurations are not part of using JIRA as a platform, but they may have a bearing in discussions between groups because changing them affects everyone. Some of the more common ones that I encounter when discussing this topic are:

- The logo and colors used by JIRA, though each JIRA project can have its own avatar or logo
- Names of system fields; any translation of a field name or status applies everywhere (Administration→Issue types, Translate)
- Whether unassigned issues are allowed or not (though if set to allowed globally this can then be set per project)
- The maximum attachment size, which is set to 10MB by default.
- Priorities; all issues use the same list of priorities in the system Priority field.
- Resolutions; all issues use the same list of resolutions in the Resolution field (this is most commonly seen during a workflow transition where they can be restricted using *Workflow Properties*).

For the last two, there is the top-voted Suggestion for JIRA (*JRA-3821*) to make priorities and resolutions fully configurable per project and issue type.

All the other system-wide configurations, such as enabling or disabling voting, can be found at Administration→System, Settings.

Worked Example: Configuring JIRA for a New Department

In this example, we're going to configure JIRA for use by an imaginary accounting department. The people in Accounting may have decided to store invoices in JIRA rather than using some other dedicated and perhaps much more expensive system.

The information stored for Accounting is totally different from what appears in a Bug issue type, and includes a custom field named "Amount." Only certain people can see the accounting information in JIRA, and some of this information is still further restricted. The accounting department also requested that they should see nothing about Engineering projects, since that was just unnecessary clutter on their screens.

The first thing to do is to take a backup of your JIRA data, do this work on a development JIRA instance, or both. The next things to do are:

1. Create a new Project Category for the accounting department, e.g., "Accounts." Some scheme names will use this word as a prefix, so make sure that the category name is something obviously unique, meaningful and brief.

2. Create a new issue type for that department's issues, for example, "Invoice." This is because we know we will have a different set of fields for accounts issues, and possibly a different workflow. Add a description of what kind of information it contains. Other scheme names will also use this word as a prefix, so make it meaningful.

3. Create a test project with a project key such as ACCTEST. JIRA project keys should generally be as brief as possible since everyone types them frequently. [1] The project name can be more descriptive than the project key. The project key and project name can be changed later on, with some restrictions such as not being able to reuse the old project key. Once this project's configuration is complete, you can create more JIRA projects and configure all of them in the same way.

---

1 You can also allow numbers and underscores in the project key if that helps. This is configured at Administration→ Settings→Advanced Settings, by clicking on the `jira.projectkey.pattern` value.

Basic JIRA Project Setup

The next stage is to do the simplest part of the job first. Edit the project configuration with Administration→Projects, then click on the project name ACCTEST (not on Edit).

Project Lead

Set the Project Lead for the project. The project lead is the person who is usually contacted to confirm future requests for changes to the project. This user will be also be the default assignee for issues in the project. With the default notification scheme, email about new issues is sent to the assignee, reporter, and watchers, so the project lead should expect to receive email about issues that were not assigned to anyone else.

Project Category

Set the Project Category for the project to the new Accounts category that we just created. Any other future accounting projects, such as ACCMAIN or ACCSUB, will also use this category.

Project Avatar

It's also a nice touch to set an avatar (a small logo) for the project to make it easy for people to quickly distinguish it from other projects. You can upload your own images. One possible idea is to use the same image for all projects in the same category for branding.

Notification Scheme

Open a new browser tab and create a new notification scheme named *Accounts Notification scheme*. Copying the Default Notification Scheme and modifying the copy is the most common way to do this. The name of this new scheme indicates what the scheme is (a notification scheme) and which category of JIRA projects it is intended for (Accounts).

In your original browser tab, set the notification scheme for the project to *Accounts Notification scheme*, using Actions→Use a different scheme.

Permission Scheme

Create a new permission scheme named *Accounts Permission scheme*. Again, copying the Default Permission Scheme and modifying the copy is the standard way to do this.

In this case, there should be no need to change any of the permissions except for one. The Set Issue Security permission controls who can change an issue's security level (see "Issue Security Schemes" on page 19). Add the Administrators role to this permission. As discussed in Chapter 1, we want to use a project role rather than a group here.

Set the permission scheme for the project to the new permission scheme, *Accounts Permission scheme*.

Groups and Roles

Define a new JIRA group named "Accounting" that contains all the users who should be able to see issues in the Accounts projects. If you're lucky, the group may already exist in your local LDAP user directory and have already been imported into JIRA.

In the project configuration page, click on View Project Roles and then:

- Delete the `jira-users` group from the Users role and add the Accounting group. Now only accounting can see the new project.
- Delete the `jira-developers` group from the Developers role and add the Accounting group.
- Add the project lead as a user to the Administrators role.

Hiding Projects from Users

At this point only Accounting users can see the Accounting projects, which is as intended, but they can still see Engineering projects. This is because all of those projects are likely using the `jira-users` group in their Users role.

To change this, we need to step back and look at how we are defining the Users role for all of the JIRA projects. The Users role is what usually controls who can access a project. There is no way to explicitly block access to a project for a specific group in JIRA. So one approach I sometimes take is that all users should be members of the default `jira-users` group, but also members of a group that controls which projects they can see.

So you might have a `mycompany-staff` group and a `contractors` group and add everyone to `jira-users` so they can log in, but change the groups in the Users role according to whether contractors have access to a particular project.

In this case I would define a group Engineering, add all the engineers to it, and then change all the Engineering projects' Users and Developers roles to use this group instead of `jira-users`.

Now the users in the Accounting group won't have access to the Engineering projects, and those projects won't clutter up JIRA for the Accounting users.

Issue Security Scheme

Create a new issue security scheme named *Accounts Issue Security scheme*:

- Add a security level named "All Accounting" and add the Accounts group to it. Make this level the default one.
- Add another security level named "Confidential Accounting" and add only a few of the accounting users who are permitted to see the more confidential accounting information.

Set the issue security scheme for the project to the new issue security scheme, *Accounts Issue Security scheme*. Now when an issue has a security level of "Confidential Accounting" only certain accounting users will be aware the issue exists.

Advanced Project Setup

Now we need to define the more complex schemes and configure the ACCTEST project to use them. These schemes are:

- Issue Type scheme
- Workflow scheme
- Field Configuration scheme
- Issue Type Screen scheme, which uses at least one Screen scheme

For most of this work, the easiest direction to work is bottom up. So create the issue type Invoice before creating an issue type scheme that uses it. And create a workflow or screen before creating the schemes that use them.

Issue Type Scheme

An Issue Type Scheme controls which issue types can be used in a project.

Under Administration→Issues, click on Issue type schemes and add a new issue type scheme named *Accounts Issue Type scheme*. Then:

- Add the main accounting issue type *Invoice* as the default issue type.
- Add other issue types, such as *Task* and *Improvement*, only if they will be used by the new department. You can reorder them to change the order in which they

appear when a user is creating an issue. The default issue type will be shown as selected at that time.

Now set the issue type scheme for the ACCTEST project to the new issue type scheme, *Accounts Issue Type scheme*.

Workflow Scheme

Create a new workflow for the Invoice issue type named *Invoice Workflow* and add the desired statuses and transitions to the new workflow. See Chapter 5 for more details on how to create a new workflow.

Create a workflow scheme named *Accounts Workflow scheme* and configure it to use the new workflow for the Invoice issue type. For any other issue types that are allowed in the project, add their workflow mappings in *Accounts Workflow scheme*. Before JIRA 5.2 if a workflow is not specified for Unassigned Types, then the default read-only JIRA workflow will be used even though the field is shown as blank. More recent versions of JIRA show the default workflow more clearly.

Set the workflow scheme for the ACCTEST project to be the new workflow scheme, *Accounts Workflow scheme*.

Field Configuration Scheme

A field configuration controls which fields are part of an issue type, e.g., what data is part of an Invoice.

Create a new field configuration named *Invoice Field Configuration*. This is *not* a scheme. Don't hide any fields here yet since we'll use screens to effectively do that later on. If a particular field is required in an Invoice issue, mark it as such here. I recommend making fields required only at the final stages of creating new schemes since it make testing harder.

Create a new field configuration scheme named *Accounts Field Configuration scheme*, and configure this new field configuration scheme to use the *Invoice Field Configuration* for the Invoice issue type.

Now set the field configuration scheme for the ACCTEST project to the new field configuration scheme, *Accounts Field Configuration scheme*.

Screen Scheme

Screens control whether a field appears in an issue to a user, and also the order in which the fields appear. Screen Schemes choose which screen is used to create, edit, or view an issue.

Create a screen named *Invoice Screen*. This screen should have all the fields that are wanted in the Invoice issue type, including the custom field Amount (after it is defined in "Adding a Custom Field" on page 38). In some versions of JIRA you can add more than one field at once, and then reorder them in one go using "Move to Position."

 I recommend starting with just one screen and using it for all three of the screens (Create, View, and Edit). Later on, you can copy and edit the screen and change the screen scheme without having to change the project settings. A good reason to have different screens is that some fields may not be known when an issue is created, or there might be fields that are not directly editable by users so should not appear on the edit screen. Another good reason is that the simpler a Create screen is, the easier it is for people to create new issues.

Create a new screen scheme named *Invoice Screen scheme* and configure the Create, Edit, and View issue screens to all be the same screen for now. This can also be done by changing the default to use just one screen.

Issue Type Screen Scheme (ITSS)

An Issue Type Screen Scheme (ITSS) ensures that the right sets of screens are used for each issue type.

Create a new ITSS named *Accounts ITSS* and configure the default screen scheme to be the *Invoice Screen scheme* defined in "Screen Scheme" on page 37. If there are other issue types, then add mappings for each one to an appropriate screen scheme. For more information about what an ITSS does, see the section "Issue Type Screen Schemes (ITSS)" on page 23.

Now set the issue type screen scheme for the ACCTEST project to the new issue type screen scheme, *Accounts ITSS*.

Adding a Custom Field

Adding a custom field is the real test of all this work, since you'll probably do it more than once for all the JIRA projects in a project category. The custom field for this example is named "Amount."

Define the new custom field with Administration→Issues→Custom fields and then the Add Custom Field link or button. This custom field is likely a Number Field. Give the field a name ("Amount") and a description. Custom field names should only use ASCII characters and should be unique to avoid confusion. Since the description appears just below the field in the issue screens, make it useful for people by describing what they are expected to enter, perhaps along with an example value. For example, *The dollar amount owed, with no dollar sign, e.g., "15.95."*

Since the accounting department will want to be able to search on this field, make sure that the Search Template value is set to something other than "None."

Now restrict the custom field to just the applicable *issue types* that uses it. For this example, that's just the Invoice issue type.

> Don't restrict the custom field to a *project* if you can avoid it, because then you'll have to come back and do that for every JIRA project that you add to the Accounts category. If you have lots of custom fields or projects, that will take you a long time to do manually.

Go to Administration→Issues→Screens and add the new custom field to the *Invoice Screen* (or to the *Invoice Create, Invoice View,* and *Invoice Edit* screens if they were defined in "Screen Scheme" on page 37). To ensure that this new field doesn't interfere with other projects and their issues, don't add the new field to any other screens, particularly not the Default screen.

This is the end of the worked example. Note that when you're looking for the Amount field to use in a simple search in the Issue Navigator, you will have to choose a project and an issue type in order for that the custom field to appear as a choice.

> Do I really have to reindex after modifying a custom field? The answer is only if the field has existing data. New fields will have their data added to the index used for searching in JIRA when issues are edited. If a custom field is only used in one project then you can reindex just that project.
>
> Prior to JIRA 5.2 reindexing used to lock all users out of JIRA until it was finished, so administrators of large JIRA instances had to wait until a convenient time occurred. Now with background indexing users can continue to use JIRA during reindexing. I still recommend reindexing at a time of low load since the process can take a long time in large JIRA instances. Until you do reindex, all JIRA administrators see a reminder about a reindex being needed in the Administration screens. Don't just reindex without thinking carefully!

Names Used in the Example

This section lists all the different names used in the example above in one convenient place:

Accounts
A project category

ACCTEST, ACCMAIN, ACCSUB
The keys of three JIRA projects in the Accounts project category

Accounting, Engineering
Groups of JIRA users

Users, Developers
The standard JIRA project roles

Invoice
A new issue type

Amount
A custom field in Invoice issues

The seven schemes and the things they control are:

Accounts Notification scheme
The notification scheme for Accounts JIRA projects

Accounts Permission scheme
The permission scheme for Accounts JIRA projects

Accounts Issue Type scheme
The issue type scheme for Accounts JIRA projects

- Invoice—a new issue type used in the ACCTEST JIRA project
- Task, Improvement— existing issue types

Accounts Issue Security scheme
The issue security scheme for Accounts JIRA projects

- All Accounting—a security level in the issue security scheme
- Confidential Accounting—another security level in the issue security scheme

Accounts Workflow scheme
> The workflow scheme for Accounts JIRA projects

>> • Invoice Workflow—a custom workflow for the Invoice issue type

Accounts Field Configuration scheme
> The field configuration scheme for Accounts JIRA projects

>> • Invoice Field Configuration—the field configuration for the Invoice issue type

Accounts ITSS
> The issue type screen scheme for Accounts JIRA projects

>> • Invoice Screen scheme—the screen scheme for the Invoice issue type

>> • Invoice Screen—the screen used for the Invoice issue type by the Invoice Screen scheme

Summary

The key to using JIRA for many groups is to have a standard way of using JIRA schemes and issue types. The details of the approach used in the example in this chapter are:

- The project category is used as the common theme for related projects.
- The naming of schemes uses the category or issue type names.
- Field constraints are implemented using issue types not projects.
- Use project roles in preference to groups.
- Document what you do!

Of course there is a balance to be struck with any approach. Too few schemes, and every change will have unwanted consequences. Too many schemes, and you risk losing track of how they differ.

 In general, try to make the names of schemes, filters and dashboards unique in their first few letters. This helps when you are searching in a long list of names. That is, don't use names such as "Agile Simplified Workflow for ..." even though JIRA Agile does.

CHAPTER 5

Creating a Workflow from Scratch

Overview

Workflows are the different statuses that an issue can have, together with the transitions between the statuses. For instance, there could be a status named *Open*, with transitions leading to the *Resolved* and *Closed* statuses.

 The word "status" is preferred over using "state" in the JIRA documentation (and also in this book), but in practice they seem to both be used interchangeably. One useful notion is that a "status" is a summary of "states." For example, someone's medical status could be summarized as "normal" based on the state of their heart, the state of their liver, and so on. In a similar way, a JIRA status is a summary of what is going on in an issue

Transitions in JIRA workflows usually go from one status to another status. However you can also define *shared* transitions (also known as *common* transitions) which go from many statuses to one status. There are also *global* transitions which go from every status to one status. Finally, *self* transitions are transitions that return to the same status they started from.

JIRA workflow transitions can also optionally have extra *triggers*, *conditions*, *validators*, and extra *post functions*:

- Triggers make the transition occur when an external event is received. This can be used for integrating JIRA with other systems.
- Conditions restrict who can see that a transition exists.

- Validators check the values that were entered during a transition. JIRA has almost no useful validators installed, but many more can be found in the recommended JIRA Suite Utilities (JSU) add-on (*http://bit.ly/1boQaKN*).

- Post functions make changes after a transition has taken place and send events to say what just happened. JIRA automatically adds certain post functions to every transition.

The statuses and transitions of the default JIRA workflow are shown in Figure 5-1, which is taken from *http://confluence.atlassian.com/display/JIRA/What+is+Workflow* and is what is seen in the Workflow Designer. The expected sequence over time goes from Open to In Progress to Resolved and Closed. Custom workflow diagrams can be customized in the workflow designer to make the expected flow more obvious.

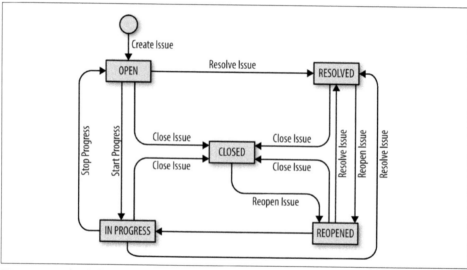

Figure 5-1. The default JIRA workflow

One of the major attractions of JIRA is the ability to customize workflows, including adding new statuses, new transitions, and making other things happen as part of transitions. This chapter describes how to create such a JIRA workflow from scratch.

Why would you want to do that? JIRA comes with one default workflow. You could create your custom workflow by simply copying and modifying the default workflow (the original is not editable). However, I've found that doing this often leads to various maintenance problems including:

- The names of your statuses may not be the same as the ones in the default JIRA workflow, and renaming them doesn't completely hide the old names everywhere in JIRA.

- The JIRA *Closed* status, by default, has a property that does not allow issues in that status to be edited (`jira.issue.editable`). It's easy to forget that the property is there until you want to bulk change many issues, some of which may be in the *Closed* status.

- The *Start Progress* transition auto-assigns the issue to the current user if permitted. This is often not what is expected.

- The *Resolved* status has a value for the system field Resolution set, even though it is not a final status. The resulting strikethrough on an issue key can be confusing for users who expect that only for Closed issues

- Some of the default JIRA transitions are *common* or *shared* transitions, meaning that changing them in one place also changes them everywhere else they are used in a workflow. This may or may not be what is wanted.

In general I recommend creating your own workflows from scratch rather than copying and modifying the default JIRA workflow.

Designing a Workflow

The hardest part about designing workflows is getting everyone to agree on them in the first place. After all the smoke and noise is over, all that is really needed is:

- The issue types that are expected to use this workflow.
- A list of the status names and their descriptions.
- A list of the transitions start and end statuses, along with transition names and descriptions.
- What, if any, information needs to be entered during each transition. Such information may be needed for restrictions of who can see or execute a transition. This information is used by the optional conditions and validators.
- Any changes to an issue other than status as part each transition. These changes are typically made using post functions.
- Any integration of the workflow with other Atlassian products using triggers.

Both statuses and transition names should be as brief, meaningful, and reusable as possible.

Some general guidelines for designing workflows that I find helpful are:

More than a dozen statuses is a large workflow
    Only use statuses that will be useful in your key reports. More statuses means more work maintaining the transitions between them all.

Use the past tense of verbs for statuses

For example "Closed," instead of "Closing" or "To Be Closed." The name of the status should describe what has *already happened* to an issue that has that status.

Use the imperative tense for transitions into a status

For example "Close," instead of "Closing" or "To Be Closed." The name of the transition should describe you want to do to the issue. You can also be explicit and name each transition "To XYZ," where "XYZ" is the name of the destination status. If there is only one transition between each status, you can even use the destination status name alone, though adding a good description for each transition is then more important.

Don't use transition names that are existing action names

There is a standard issue action called "Assign" that assigns an issue to a different user. If you give a transition that same name, then your users will see two tabs on an issue, both named "Assign," that do very different things. Avoid confusing your users and don't use "Assign" as a transition name.

Fewer statuses is better

Use the smallest number of statuses possible. More than about ten suggests you may have overcomplicated the workflow, which in turn means that other people will have a hard time using it. You may need to have more than one issue type and a workflow for each issue type.

One way to decide whether you need a status is to consider whether any report that actually matters would use it, and whether that same information can perhaps be provided by JIRA in a different way.

Clear descriptions

Make sure that you have a brief description of the purpose of every status and transition, and enter it the JIRA workflow. This will appear as a floating tooltip on transitions to guide confused users.

Put statuses and transitions in their expected order

Whenever you list the statuses during design or are adding them to a JIRA workflow, do so in the order that you expect them to appear most of the time, in a vertical stack. The use of a vertical stack makes the expected path through a workflow clearer. This is particularly true for earlier versions of JIRA or when using the text-based workflow editor. Similarly, add the most common transition first in any list of transitions from a status. An alternative way to change the order that transitions appear using transition properties such as opsbar-sequence is described at *https://confluence.atlassian.com/display/JIRA/Workflow +Properties*. If you're not using JIRA Cloud you can even export the workflow XML, change the order of the transitions and reimport the modified XML (in a test JIRA first).

Workflow screens

A transition can either happen immediately, or a transition screen with various fields on it can be shown during the transition. Transition screens also have a place to leave a comment about why the transition was made. JIRA provides two standard screens for this (Resolve Issue screen and Workflow screen), but if there are fields that you want to allow to be edited during a transition, then you can define your own screens. Just don't use the Default screen as a transition screen, because when users change statuses they'll feel rather overwhelmed by seeing *all* of the fields in the issue. A good transition screen presents the user with the fields that are most commonly changed during a particular transition.

Which statuses are resolved?

Decide which statuses should always have a value set in the system Resolution field (Chapter 2). Make sure that all transitions from a non-resolved status to a resolved status set the Resolution, and that all transitions from resolved to non-resolved statuses clear the resolution. Otherwise you'll see reopened issues with a strikethrough in their issue keys.

Allow for mistakes: no status is final

Every status should have a transition to another status: otherwise, it becomes a final status. Final statuses are fine until someone accidentally moves an issue into one and then can't undo their mistake. You can always allow only administrators to execute a transition if you want to make it more difficult to change a status.

The workflow shown in Figure 5-2 is an improved version of Figure 5-1. It was drawn with the Gliffy drawing tool, which is available as a add-on for both JIRA and Confluence (*https://marketplace.atlassian.com/plugins/com.gliffy.integration.jira*). The points to notice are that the most common path through the workflow is a vertical stack of statuses. Other less common statuses such as Reopened are off to the side. Statuses that expect to have a resolution set are shown with a heavier border (Resolved, Closed). If I were further refining this workflow, I would remove the Reopened status since the same information about whether an issue has been reopened can be gathered with the JQL was operator, e.g., `status = Open and status was Closed`.

For many workflows, I find that thinking about the intended assignee and their team for each status is helpful when designing the workflow. For instance, a bug might have been assigned to a default user for a project, then to a developer, then to QA for testing, and finally assigned to someone in Operations for deployment as part of a release. I try to consider what each person will want to do most frequently with the issue.

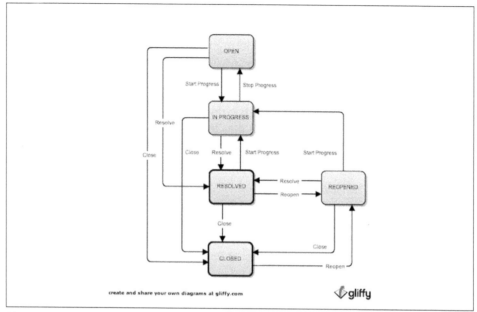

Figure 5-2. An Improved Default JIRA workflow

JIRA Agile and Workflows

JIRA Agile (*https://www.atlassian.com/software/jira/agile*), formerly known as *Green-Hopper*, is a popular JIRA add-on by Atlassian that allows you to manage issues in a more agile way. This means Kanban, Scrum, sprints, burndown charts, and a whiteboard-like active sprints board where you can drag issues from status to status. You don't even have to be working in an agile way to appreciate it. So it's very popular indeed.

JIRA Agile "cards" are simply JIRA issues displayed differently, so of course each card uses a JIRA workflow. The difference is that JIRA Agile lets you assign multiple statuses to *columns* on the Active Sprints (Work) board. For example, the column named "To Do" could have issues in the "Open" and "Reopened" statuses. When designing a workflow for use in a JIRA Agile board, there are a few points to remember.

Columns

Define the names for your JIRA Agile columns and decide which JIRA statuses should be mapped to each column. You can have statuses that don't map to any of your columns, and in fact this is sometimes a useful way to keep issues from appearing on a board.

Transitions

If you want to be able to drag an issue from any column to any other column, you will need to have a transition from every status to every other status. A regular JIRA workflow is often shaped like a ladder or diagonal, but a workflow for use in JIRA Agile is more like a fully connected circle. You'll at least need a transition to one of the statuses in every column to allow cards to be dragged. This is an $O(N^2)$ number of transitions. A better approach is to define a common transition for entering each status. That way you only have to define as many as the number of statuses in the workflow.

The *Agile Simplified* workflows that JIRA Agile can create are just the statuses with a *global* transition to every status. This means that you'll see transitions back to the same status in every issue which can confuse some users. You also need to check that the system Resolution field is set properly in these generated workflows.

You can add multiple conditions to a transition and even have levels of combinations of them. However I recommend avoiding complicated conditions that restrict who can change an issue's status, or you'll have users who are frustrated that they can drag issues to some columns but not other columns.

Transition Screens

Many people like to avoid transition screens with JIRA Agile. When they're dragging issues from one screen to another, they don't want to have pop-ups interrupting them. This is fine except for transitions that need to set a resolution. The resolution can be set in a post function, but which resolution to choose? I recommend choosing the most frequent resolution, then add another transition between the same two statuses with a transition screen that lets you choose a resolution. When the issue is dragged to a column where the resolution should be set, two small areas will appear named after each transition. One could be "Completed" since it sets the resolution with no pop-up screen, and the other could be named something such as "Close - Other."

Notifications

People drag issues around on the work board without realizing that they are sending out email about status changes. You may want to use a custom event for some transitions and prevent the notification scheme from sending out email for that event.

Implementing a Workflow

Once you have the names and descriptions of the statuses and transitions, you can create the new workflow at Administration→Issues→Workflows. For ideas on naming the workflow, see the sections "Workflow Schemes" on page 21 and "Workflow Scheme" on page 37.

JIRA has included some kind of graphical workflow designer since version 4.4. To use the text-based editor in JIRA 5 you have to click on the column that shows the number of steps in a workflow or the Text link. Since JIRA 6, there is a more obvious Text button to allow users to work with the text editor.

The graphical editor is an improvement on the original workflow editor, which had also some limitations about what it could do with draft workflows (see "Further Reading" on page 54). I confess I still create and edit workflows using the original text editor though, perhaps from long familiarity. However there's no other way than the Workflow Designer to produce workflow diagrams.

First, create new statuses as necessary at Administration→Issues→Statuses, or in the graphical designer Statuses area.

If you are not using the graphical workflow designer, then add the statuses to the workflow in the expected order of their most frequent use.

 A workflow is actually made up of *steps*, and each step has just one *status* associated with it. For simplicity make the step names the same as the status names—otherwise, your users will see discontinuities in a few places in JIRA.

JIRA will have added a first step named "Open." After you add other steps you will be able to make any one of them your initial status, and can then delete the original step that JIRA added for you. To change the initial status, click on the Open step name, then the Create Issue transition, then Edit, and finally change the Destination Step to the new initial status.

Next, add the transitions away from the first status, also in their expected order of use.

For each transition, after you've entered the name and description, check which triggers, conditions, validators, and post functions are wanted, and add them. If you see a number after a transition name, that's a unique ID for that transition. This can help to see which transitions are shared (common) or global

I recommend changing the event fired in the post function from Generic Event to something more informative, even if it's only Issue Updated. This can also be used reduce the amount of email sent when an issue is updated as described in "Workflows and Events" on page 53.

Check that there is a Transition permission condition. This controls who can change the status of an issue. Earlier versions of JIRA didn't restrict this except by adding a condition to each transition. In that case I recommend adding a Permission Condition to check for Edit permission and make this behave as expected. Adding such a condition also makes it easier to make a JIRA project properly read-only.

You are allowed to have "self" transitions back to the same status if you want to. This is one way to narrowly restrict what is changed in an issue, and is used in the section "Resolution" on page 8.

The default JIRA workflow has some triggers, conditions, validators, and post functions that are worth knowing about:

- The initial Create Issue transition into Open has a validator to check that the user has the Create Issues permission.
- Transitions have a condition that checks for the Transition Issues permission.
- The Start Progress transition has a condition to check that the current user is the issue's assignee. Other users won't see this transition as a choice. Other variants of the default workflow assign the issue to the current user during this transition.
- The Closed status has the `jira.issue.editable` property set to `false` which means that issues with this status can't be edited.
- Many statuses and transitions have a property `jira.i18n.title` which is used to get the actual name. If you're having problems renaming something, look for this property, and either delete it or translate the status' name at Administration→Issues→Statuses.

There are five post functions that are added by default to new transitions, but only one of these is editable: "Fire Generic Event." Events are discussed later in "Workflows and Events" on page 53.

Deploying and Testing a Workflow

When a workflow is created from scratch, there is of course no project or issue type that is using it, so it's *inactive*. Recent versions of JIRA display workflows in active and inactive sections, and the inactive section is not expanded. If you can't find the workflow you just created, expand the inactive section before searching for it on your browser page.

The first step towards making a workflow active is to create a workflow scheme to define which issue types use each workflow. For instance, tasks (issues with issue type *Task*) could have a different workflow from bugs, which have an issue type of *Bug*. See "Workflow Scheme" on page 37 for details on a recommended way to do this.

Once you have a workflow scheme that refers to the new workflow, you can edit a JIRA project to use the workflow scheme (go to Administration→Projects and click on the project name). Then go to Workflows and click Switch Scheme.

Now when you create a new issue of the specified type in that project, you should see that the status of the issue is the one that you chose as the initial status. The available workflow choices for the issue should be the transitions that you defined as possible from that status. The permission View Read-only Workflow allows people to see an image of each issue's workflow. This is so helpful that it's worth adjusting the workflow diagram in the graphical editor to make it clearer.

To test the workflow, execute the transitions between all the statuses, checking for usability errors as well as any actual failures or error messages in the JIRA log files. Check that any custom triggers, conditions, validators, or post functions behave as expected. Manually testing all the different combinations of transitions and user permissions is only really possible for small to medium-sized workflows.

To make a change to a workflow once it is in use and active, you have to create a draft of the workflow (the graphical designer will do this automatically), edit the draft, and finally publish the draft. The option of saving a copy of the original workflow is offered when the workflow is published, and can be useful if version numbers are added to the workflow name. However, I generally find it leads to too many copies of old workflows, so I don't use it very often.

Some changes to a workflow can't be done by creating a draft. For the following changes you have to create a copy of the workflow, edit the inactive copy and then change the workflow scheme to use the copy.

- A workflow's name cannot be changed, though the description can.
- Statuses cannot be removed.
- A status can only have new transitions added from it if it already has at least one outgoing transition. So dead-end statuses cannot have an outgoing transition added.
- Changing the name of a step used for a status. Generally the step name should be the same as the status name.

One thing that's currently missing in JIRA is a way to compare two versions of the same workflow. When I really want to be sure of what has changed, I export the workflow's XML before and after the change and then compare the two files using a *diff* tool, preferably one that understands XML.

Workflows and Events

JIRA sends software "events" internally when issues are changed. Some of these events are hardcoded, such as the one sent when an issue's assignee changes. However, events sent during a transition are designed to be configurable. Many of the events listed at Administration→System→Events are really intended for use in workflows. For example, the "Work Started on Issue" event is intended to be sent ("fired") by a post function on all transitions into the "In Progress" status.

The standard post function "Fire Generic Event" can be edited to send a more appropriate event when a transition executes. The main reason that a JIRA administrator cares about what type of events are sent is because they are used by a project's Notification Scheme (see "Notification Schemes" on page 16), which controls who receives email when the status of an issue changes.

You can also add new types of events to JIRA at Administration→System→Events, as described in detail at *http://confluence.atlassian.com/display/JIRA/Adding+a+Custom +Event*.

The ability to create new events and have your workflow fire them off instead of the Generic event or some other standard event can be useful for trimming JIRA spam. For example, if you really want to fine-tune who receives email when an issue changes status, you can define a new event type for each transition, perhaps giving them highly descriptive names such as *Task Workflow: Open to Resolved Event*. (The event names don't appear in email templates.) Then you can edit the transition from Open to Resolved, and change its post function to fire the appropriate new event. In a custom notification scheme, you can then specify which users will receive email for precisely that one transition and no other transitions.

Transitions, Sub-Tasks, and Links

When designing a workflow, there is often some confusion over which parts of JIRA are best for different purposes. Should a task be tracked as a sub-task of the main task? What are the differences between sub-tasks and links for reporting? This section clarifies the advantages and disadvantages of different ways of designing workflows.

A transition is part of a linear flow in a JIRA workflow. It doesn't have support for parallel actions. Transitions are intended to be relatively simple, perhaps with some post functions that set values in an issue.

Standard JIRA supports two levels of hierarchy in issues, and just one level of hierarchy for projects. An issue of type Bug or any other issue type can have many sub-issues. The Sub-task is just one of many possible sub-issue types. The only difference between an issue and a sub-issue is that the sub-issue has a value in its Parent field.

The advantage of a sub-task is that work can be recorded independently of the parent issue. So if two pieces of work proceed in parallel, they may be a good fit for using sub-issues. Sub-issues and their progress are displayed clearly inside the parent issue. Sub-tasks can be searched for with JQL such as: `parent in ("TEST-2")`. Sub-issues have to be in the same project as their parent issue.

Issue links are a more general form of sub-tasks because they allow a many-to-many relationship. You can also choose different types of links such as "Related To" or "Duplicate." You can further customize issue links by defining your own link types. Issue links are visible from inside issues, and can now be searched in JQL with: `key in linkedIssues("TEST-2")`. JIRA does not have a general purpose tool to display the relationship between a set of linked issues, but there at least two add-ons that provide this: Links Explorer (*http://bit.ly/ZFl9QO*) and Links Hierarchy Structure (*http://bit.ly/13S5YDv*).

Neither sub-issues nor links can be easily ordered in JIRA. That is, the related issues are a set, not a queue. Also, sub-tasks inherit the issue security setting of their parent issue.

JIRA Agile (*https://www.atlassian.com/software/jira/agile*) adds an *Epic* issue type which provides a way to collect issues together. This is the most common way to add another hierarchy level to JIRA.

If you need more levels of hierarchy than JIRA and JIRA Agile provide then you may be interested in the Structure add-on from ALM Works (*http://bit.ly/11bbYFs*), which provides multiple levels for JIRA issues with a well-integrated UI.

Further Reading

The documentation for configuring workflows can be found at *http://confluence.atlas sian.com/display/JIRA/Configuring+Workflow*.

The process of changing a workflow so that issues in the Closed status can be edited is described at *http://confluence.atlassian.com/display/JIRA/Allow+editing+of+Closed +Issues*.

The limitations of how draft workflows can be changed using the original workflow editor are documented at *https://confluence.atlassian.com/display/JIRA/Configuring +Workflow#ConfiguringWorkflow-Limitations*.

Details of adding a new event to JIRA are at *http://confluence.atlassian.com/display/ JIRA/Adding+a+Custom+Event*.

CHAPTER 6

Custom Fields

Overview

One of the primary purposes of an issue tracker is to collect organized data, and custom fields let you personalize that data. If you need to track how many angels can dance on the head of a pin, JIRA allows you to create a custom field for that. (It would be a number field, presumably, though number field values in JIRA have an upper limit of 100 trillion.) The appeal of creating custom fields is understandable, and it makes sense that as an organization grows and adopts JIRA for varied purposes, the number of custom fields grows along with it.

The problem is that custom fields are like glazed doughnuts—they always seem like a good idea at the time, but if you continue thinking that way in perpetuity then you're sure to witness a reduction in speed. The number of custom fields in JIRA is one of the most significant factors in the performance of a JIRA instance. You can see the details of Atlassian's performance testing of JIRA 6.4 in their enterprise documentation at *https://confluence.atlassian.com/display/ENTERPRISE/Scaling+JIRA*.

There are certainly other factors that can affect performance, such as the number of issues, number of concurrent users, and behavior (or lack thereof) of add-ons. But for most administrators, many of these factors are difficult to directly control. Managing the number of custom fields in your instance is the most straightforward way to control the performance of JIRA.

In addition to improving performance, custom field management can help reduce the administrative overhead involved in updating and maintaining custom fields in JIRA. Restricting the overall number of fields is only part of this process. Care and thought should be put into the selection of custom field types and how those fields are configured. This will pay dividends for your users in terms of reporting and user experience.

What's the Big Deal with Custom Fields?

When users think of the fields associated with an issue, they think of the fields that are actually displayed on the screen for that issue. JIRA thinks differently. When a new custom field is created in JIRA, by default it is added to every JIRA project and issue type, even if it never actually appears on a screen. This means that JIRA has to make a decision about that custom field for most issue operations such as create, edit, and search, even when the field has no value. The part of JIRA most impacted by all this additional work is the Lucene issue index.

The Lucene index is your database's butler. It maintains its own copy of all of JIRA's issue information in a format that is optimized for search operations. When you submit a JQL search it is the Lucene index, not the database, that handles the request. This significantly reduces the load on the database and is the reason the database is rarely a performance bottleneck for JIRA, and that most JIRA searches are surprisingly fast. You can delete the Lucene index and rebuild it from the information in the database (though it may take a while in larger JIRA instances, so be careful).

To understand the impact of custom fields on the Lucene index it helps to visualize the Lucene index as a spreadsheet where issues are along the y axis and custom fields are along the x axis, as shown in Figure 6-1. Scaling along either direction (by adding an issue or a custom field) increases the complexity of searching for issues. Keep in mind that the Lucene index has to be kept synchronized with the data. This means that whenever the data is updated, the index needs to be updated as well. This is why creating, editing, and searching issues all impact the index. As more custom fields are added to JIRA, the time it takes to complete any of these operations increases.

	A	B	C	D	E	F	G	H
	Issue Key	Summary	Description	...	Custom Field A	Custom Field B	...	Custom Field ZZ
	TEST-123	My first issue	Lots of text here		Ops team	2		London
	TEST-222	Another issue	Text text text		Eng team	45		Palo Alto
	(more issues)							

Figure 6-1. Visualizing information in the Lucene issues index

If you are administering a large JIRA instance, it is important to understand this relationship between custom fields, the Lucene index, and performance. This can prove helpful in troubleshooting, especially if you notice a lot of activity reading from and writing to the disk where the index lives. Note that Atlassian recommends using a fast, local disk for the Lucene index files. More commonly, you should be exercising this knowledge to guide your decisions about how you set up and configure custom fields.

If you are administering a small JIRA instance, then you are unlikely to notice any performance benefits from reducing the number of custom fields below a few hundred. Small JIRA instances often experience no real performance issues at all. However, as I mentioned in the introduction, there's more to managing custom fields than just performance benefits.

Choosing Custom Field Types

JIRA ships with 22 custom field types.[1] The following list includes the other 20 types along with discussion about when to use each one. Add-ons can provide you with many other custom field types, see their documentation for more information about those.

Standard Text Fields

Standard text fields contain text. No surprises, no strings attached! (Okay, technically they have nothing but strings attached.) The standard text fields all use the *Free Text Searcher*. This means that a general JQL text search such as text ~ "foo" will search in all the custom text fields as well as the system text fields (Summary, Description, Environment, and Comments).

Text Field (single line)
This field has a practical limit of 254 characters. This is your best choice if the information you are trying to capture is short. Compared to multiline text fields, single line text fields have a smaller screen footprint, which is good for the interface.

Text Field (multiline)
JIRA does not limit the size of multiline text fields. Because of this, the theoretical limit is derived from the kind of database that JIRA is using. In practice you will break the interface before you exceed the limit.

The Description system field is a multiline text field, and if you can search for any information within that field. You could keep all your unstructured text about an issue just in the Description and Comments fields. However, it is sometimes useful to have other multiline text fields to help people know what information to add where.

Text Field (read only)
The read only text field has a limit of 255 characters. It can be configured to appear on view screens but not on create, edit, or transition screens. This means

---

1 Two of these (*Hidden Job Switch* and *Job Checkbox*) only apply to the Perforce integration (*http://www.perforce.com*), so I am choosing to ignore them.

it cannot be used to display messages to your users on these screens, which limits its value somewhat. You also cannot assign the field a default value. The value can be set using a post function, so the field can be used to set a value in a workflow when you don't want the any one to edit that field. This field is most often used to hold read-only information about issues imported into JIRA from other systems.

Validated Free Input Fields

These fields have a text input box where you can enter whatever you please; however, JIRA will only accept certain values.

Number Field

Not surprisingly, JIRA will only accept a value in this field if it is a number and formatted in the appropriate way for your JIRA locale. Decimals are fine, but are rounded to three decimal places. Negative values are also allowed. The upper limit, as mentioned in the introduction to this chapter, is 100 trillion. The lower limit is peculiar to say the least. Suffice to say that I've gotten JIRA to output a value of negative infinity. Also, searching on a range of negative numbers returns confusing results.

URL

This is a single line text field that will only accept a URL. What this means is that the value is checked to ensure that a valid protocol has been entered (e.g., `http://`) followed by other characters.

The URL searcher is an exact text searcher, which is rather unfortunate. This means you cannot do a text search to find all addresses with "oreilly" in the URL. You have to search for the full URL text such as `http://shop.oreilly.com/cate gory/new.do`. The URL field also suffers from a field limit of 255 characters, which can be frustrating when dealing with longer URLs.

Option Fields

Option fields allow the user to select from a predefined discrete list of choices. This makes them the best choice for getting consistent, reportable field values without having to worry about the case sensitivity and spelling variations of the Labels field (see "The Labels Field" on page 59).

Select List (single choice)

Single choice select lists allow the user to choose just one value from a list of options. If this is the desired behavior, then this is your field. Be careful, though, there is no easy way to convert custom field types. You cannot simply convert this field into a multiselect list later.

Select List (multiple choices)

Unlike its single-select relative, a multiple choice select list (multiselect list) allows you to choose as many options as are available. If you are torn between whether to use a single or multiselect list, then in general you should go with the multiselect list because it is more flexible.

Select List (cascading)

A cascading select list actually consists of two single select lists where the options in the second list depend on what is chosen in the first list. This mechanism is an excellent way to break down long lists of choices that can be logically categorized with the first list. The timezone options in your JIRA user profile are an excellent example of a cascading select list. There are no options to add additional cascades, nor are there cascading multiselect lists.

Note that if you make a cascading select list required with a field configuration, as in "Field Configuration Schemes" on page 21, only the first list requires a value. The *None* option will still be available for the second list.

Radio Buttons

A radio button field is functionally identical to a single select list. Choosing one over the other simply boils down to cosmetic preference. I personally have a strong preference for the single select list because it is more compact on the screen, but only if you have a small number of options like "Yes" and "No."

Checkboxes

Here we have another repeat because checkboxes are functionally identical to a multiselect list. This time, however, I have no favorite. I find that the interface for checkboxes is cleaner and more intuitive, while multiselect lists should always be used when you have many options. If I know that the list of options will always be small (say six or fewer), then I consider using checkboxes.

The Labels Field

The labels field is special enough to get its own section. Labels are the same idea as "tags" in many other applications. This field type combines the reportable nature of option fields with the freedom of text fields. Labels are best used for short-term work by a small set of users. This allows users to quickly gather data on a collection of issues without requiring the creation of a new custom field or options.

Because anyone can create a new label, it's very easy to create multiple labels for the same thing. For example, were all those issues labeled with *HP* or *Hewlett_Packard*? Even with JIRA prompting them with existing values, people tend to mistype the same word over time. To make matters more confusing, labels are case-sensitive when they are added but case-insensitive when searching for issues by label.

JIRA labels cannot contains spaces, and cannot easily be renamed in bulk or deleted. As of JIRA 6.4, bulk updates to issues can now append to Labels field values instead of overwriting the existing values.

Labels
> If you want another field that functions exactly like the system Labels field, you can create a custom labels field. While the system Labels field very effectively fills a niche purpose, adding a second labels field provides little additional value, and I have rarely found use for one. One benefit of a custom labels field is that its values (and hence the values that appear in its drop-down list) are independent of the system Labels field.

Date Picker Fields

Date fields are critical to how users sort and plan their work in JIRA. Adding custom date fields can make a crucial difference for teams with sensitive time-based requirements.

Date Picker
> The date picker allows you to choose a specific day but not a specific time on that day. This works well if the time is irrelevant.
>
> The date picker field does not seem to have any clear value limits. If you plan on sticking to dates within 1970 to 2030, you should be fine, but I wouldn't use JIRA to date ancient artifacts or plan a timeline for interstellar travel.

Date Time Picker
> As the name implies, this field allows you to choose both a date and a time. This field is most often used to capture the time when a certain event, such as a workflow transition, occurred.
>
> Date time fields are stored as Unix timestamps and will not behave properly for dates before January 1st, 1970 or after January 19th, 2038 (UTC).

When you use JQL to search for dates, remember that if you just specify a date then JIRA assumes that you mean *midnight* at the start of that day. For example, if you want to find issues with a due date of 9th July 2015 and earlier, you have to search for `duedate <= '2015/07/09 23:59'` or just `duedate < '2015/07/10'`.

User & Group Picker Fields

User Picker and Group Picker fields can also be incredibly useful. You can use them to create new issue-specific roles[2] such as *Tester* or *Approver*. These custom user fields can be referenced in permission schemes, notification schemes and workflows, giving administrators tremendous flexibility to shape the way that users interact with issues.

User Picker (single user)
    The single user picker is a great choice for an issue role that would only ever have a single user in it (e.g., QA Lead).

User Picker (multiple users)
    Multiuser pickers allow us to choose multiple users for an issue role without needing them to be in the same group. This custom field type really shines for listing a set of reviewers, testers, or approvers of an issue. The multiuser picker is also your answer to allowing multiple assignees on an issue. I typically keep the Assignee field as the primary responsible user, and list other assignees in an *Additional Assignees* multiuser picker field.

Group Picker (single group)
    The single group picker allows you to select a JIRA group instead of a JIRA user. This provides one possible solution to the problem of how to assign a team to an issue, assuming that your teams can be maintained as directory groups. (The other solution is to use an option field, but a group field is the more powerful of the two.)

Be incredibly wary of adding a group field to your notification schemes. Without validation, there is nothing to stop a user from adding the `jira-users` group to the custom group field and notifying all of your JIRA users. This particular *faux pas* is a likely way to earn an unhappy conversation with your boss. Using a group picker in a permission scheme has no such risk, however.

---

2 This is unrelated to a *project* role.

Group Picker (multiple groups)
Like all multipicker fields, the multigroup picker is more versatile than the single-select version. See the entry for the single group picker for the warning about referencing this field in a notification scheme.

Other Picker Fields

These fields types allow you to choose from other objects in JIRA, specifically versions and projects.

Version Picker (single version)
A version picker lets you selects from all available versions for an issue's project, just as the Affects Versions and Fix Versions system fields do. The single version picker differs from the system fields in that it only allows the selection of a single version. Because JIRA has a great deal of built-in functionality surrounding the system version fields (especially the Fix Versions field), I don't recommend trying to replace them. Only use custom version fields to supplement the existing system fields, for example a version field named "Target Fix Version" is sometimes used.

Version Picker (multiple versions)
This field type behaves the same as the system version fields except that there is no built-in functionality for it. It does not appear in release notes (*https://conflu ence.atlassian.com/display/JIRA/Creating+Release+Notes*) nor does it contribute to version progress in JIRA's roadmap feature.

Project Picker (single project)
The project picker allows a user to choose from any project that is visible to them. While this field is rarely useful in most projects, it is very useful in a JIRA administration project, e.g., "What project is related to your issue?"

There is a long-standing bug where the *merge function* for version pickers custom fields does not work as expected. When a merge is performed on a particular version, that value is deleted from a custom version field instead of updated. This is even more reason to stick with the system version fields.

What is a Custom Field Context?

A custom field context controls the scope, default value, and certain type-specific features for a custom field in JIRA. Before addressing the details of contexts, though, I'll address the matter of what this feature is called.

The custom field context is known by several names in different places in JIRA. The two most common names are "custom field context" and "custom field configuration scheme." Other names are a combination of the first, e.g., "configuration scheme context." I have a strong preference for the term *custom field context*. "Custom field configuration scheme" is too easily confused with "field configuration scheme," which is one of the seven schemes of JIRA discussed in "Field Configuration Schemes" on page 21. For this reason, I'll use the term *custom field context*, or simply *context*, throughout this chapter.

To access custom field contexts, go to Administration → Issues → Custom fields, click on the custom field name, and then click on *Configure* under the cog item on the right. You should see a screen similar to the one shown in Figure 6-2. (*Edit* is for changing a field name, description or searcher, but not for contexts.)

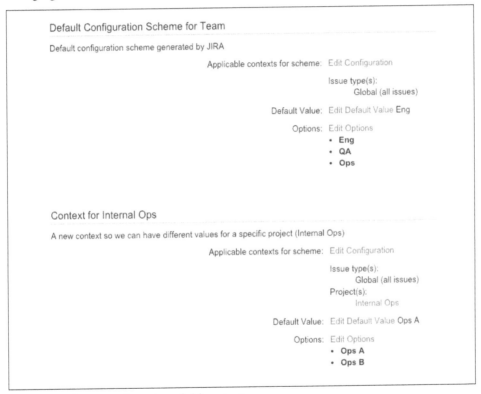

Figure 6-2. An example custom field context

The context is where you can usually set the default value for any custom field. This is useful for setting list options to the most common value or for adding a template or help text to a text field.

For option fields, the context allows you to edit the option list, whether this is for renaming options, disabling or deleting options, or adding new options to the list of options. Deleting an option that has been used in JIRA constitutes data loss, so make such a change with care and read "Deleting Contexts" on page 66 carefully before-hand.

Single user picker fields can optionally have user filtering applied at their context. This allows you to restrict the set of valid users for such a field by groups and project roles. For example you could restrict the options for a *QA Lead* single user picker custom field to only accept members of a Quality Assurance project role.

Limiting Contexts

The default context created for all new custom fields is a *global* context. This means that upon creation, the field is potentially applicable to all projects and issue types in JIRA. By editing the configuration of the context, you can limit which projects and issue types it will actually appear in. An issue whose project and issue type are outside the scope of a field's context will not display that field, even if it is on the correct screen and remains shown by the field configuration.

The ability to control context is useful when you need to add a field to a commonly used screen for only a few projects or issue types.

For example, let's say that you would like to categorize bug fixes with a custom field named "Bug Category" that has options like "Unhandled Exception," "UI Error," "Logic Error," and so on. The logical time to set this field would be during the resolution of the issue, but the field is only meaningful for issues of type Bug.

In this scenario, let's assume that the project you want to modify has several issue types that are using the same screens and workflow. Without using contexts, you would have to take the following steps to implement the requirements for the new field:

1. Copy the transition screen being used to set the resolution in the workflow.
2. Add the Bug Category field to the new transition screen.
3. Copy the workflow to a new workflow for Bug issues.
4. Edit the new workflow to use the new transition screen.
5. Update the workflow scheme for the project to use the new workflow for Bug issues.

The need to "fork" the workflow means that you now have another workflow to maintain for this JIRA project. If your users need to be able to view or edit this field, you would need to add new screens and screen schemes, further complicating the configuration.

The solution using contexts is much more elegant. You simply limit the context to the Bug issue type only, then add the field to all screens where it is wanted. The field will then show only for the Bug issue type.

Another advantage of using custom field contexts is that they can actually improve JIRA's performance. Part of this benefit comes from eliminating the schemes that you would have otherwise needed. But the actual narrowing of the context has a direct impact on the Lucene index. When a field's context is limited, the Lucene index marks that field as unsearchable for everything outside of its context. This can improve search times because JIRA is able to skip the processing of irrelevant fields.

Adding Contexts

The most glorious aspect of custom field contexts is that you can have multiple contexts for a single custom field. For a given custom field you could create a different context for each project and set each one to have a different default value. By far though, this feature is most useful for allowing option fields to list different options for each context (project and issue type). Because of this flexibility, it is recommended to give custom fields as generic a name as possible. This will allow you to more easily reuse custom fields across JIRA, while minimizing the number of total custom fields.

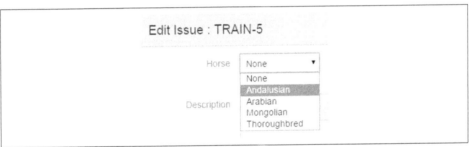

Figure 6-3. The TRAIN project is using the default global context that lists Horse options as breeds

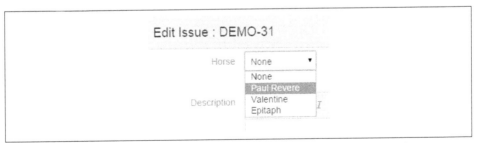

Figure 6-4. The DEMO project is using the same custom field but with a different context that lists Horse options by their names

There are limits to how contexts can be used. Each JIRA project can only have a single context, and each field can only have a single global context. A project-specific context will override a global context. This effectively means that you can never have different option values for different issue types within the same project.

Dangers of Custom Field Contexts

Making changes to JIRA's seven schemes is like being guided across a crosswalk by a giant fuzzy teddy bear. Sure, there is some inherent danger, but the path is clear and you have a friend looking out for you. By contrast, making changes to custom field contexts is like being guided across a tightrope by a grizzly bear. As long as you are careful, everything will be fine, but things sure can go sour quickly.

Deleting Contexts

 Read this section and the next *before* you delete or change a context for an Options custom field!

Deleting a context in JIRA is frighteningly easy. It takes only a single click on the trash can icon next to a context, and there is no confirmation screen or warning. This is not a problem for text fields, but for Options fields it effectively removes all of the data from issues that were using the deleted context. The data will be visible in affected issues until you try to edit the issue—then the options from the new context will be shown, and the old value is gone. The old value is shown in the issue's History tab.

Changing Contexts

Unlike deleting contexts, editing contexts is a regularly occurring operation for JIRA administrators that use them. In the course of editing a context you may accidentally remove projects or issue types that were previously using that context. If the change results in a project or issue type having no context, there is little danger. The data will still be present and the context simply needs to be edited to include that project or issue type again. However if the context has actually changed (perhaps by defaulting to the global context, and is for an Options field), then you are up against the clock: now, editing an issue will force the user to choose a value from the new context. Even if the user doesn't choose a new value, the old value will be cleared. Hence, the longer this change goes unrepaired, the more data you could lose.

Adding a New Context

Options in different contexts with the same option name are still unique because they have different numeric identifiers. That is, an option named "Dog" in one context is not the same as an option also named "Dog" in another context, even though their names are the same.

So adding a new context with the same option names as the previous context still means you are changing contexts. This will not be immediately obvious because searching will find both the new and the old option name and they will be lumped together in your search results, but they are still inherently different values. Editing any issue with an old context will drop the value unless the new value is selected.

Screens and Field Configurations and Custom Field Contexts, Oh My!

So far in this book we've seen three different ways to control fields in JIRA. Table 6-1 contains a review of what screens ("Issue Type Screen Schemes (ITSS)" on page 23), field configurations ("Field Configuration Schemes" on page 21), and custom field contexts do.

Table 6-1. Screens, field configurations, and custom field contexts

Feature	Screens	Field configurations	Custom field contexts
Granularity	Per operation per issue type per project	Per issue type per project	Per project, and enable/disable per issue type
Show fields	✓		
Hide fields	✓ (custom fields only on view screen)	✓	✓ (custom fields only)
Change field descriptions		✓	
Change text renderers		✓	
Make fields required		✓ (see note)	
Set/change default values			✓ (custom fields only)
Change option values			✓ (custom fields only)

 The Assignee, Comment, and Attachment fields can't be made required. Issue Type and Summary fields are always required. The Resolution field is required in transition screens.

Table 6-1 shows what is unique about each feature. If you need a field to be displayed in an issue, it must be on a screen. To make a field required, set its renderer, or change its description from the default, then you must use a field configuration. And custom field contexts are the only way to set and change default fields values or option field values.

In fact, the only overlapping functionality between the three features is that they can all be used to hide fields. On this matter, there is no clear winner among them. Each has its own advantages and disadvantages for hiding fields. Deciding between them is largely a matter of figuring out which one would require the fewest number of configurations to enforce the required behavior.

For instance, screens have the best granularity of the three options, as you can use a different screen for create, edit, view, and transition operations all within the same issue. So if you need a field to show on an issue only at certain times, you should use screens to control the field's presence. I also recommend using separate screens when they serve separate purposes. While you can use elaborate field configurations and contexts to enable you to reuse a screen in highly disparate issue types, at some point it becomes easier to maintain two separate screens than a multitude of strange field configurations.

 Note that excluding a field from a screen does not make it invalid for the issue type, and any valid field can be edited through the bulk change operation.

Field configurations are the only way to hide system fields. If you need to hide one of the system fields that stubbornly refuses to disappear from the view screen (e.g., the Labels field) then you must use a field configuration. Field configurations are also the only feature where hiding a field is the active option. That is, hiding a field using screens or contexts is passive—they hide fields by exclusion. This means that ideally, field configurations should be used only to hide a field that rarely needs to be hidden, as that will minimize the number of overall configurations needed (as well as the effort to maintain those configurations).

Using custom field contexts to hide fields does have performance benefits, but those benefits are slight. More emphasis should be put on using contexts appropriately than trying to eke every last performance benefit out of JIRA. The question then becomes a matter of how often the field will be used. If the field is unique to only a few projects or issue types, then contexts are a good choice for hiding the field. In this scenario, you will only rarely need to modify the context when new projects and issue types are added, as the field will generally be inapplicable to most of them.

In summary, you should create a unique set of screens for each broad type of work that your organization is tracking in JIRA. This is also discussed in Chapter 4.

- If there are unique situations that need a field to be hidden for a minority of projects, use a field configuration to hide it and avoid creating a duplicate set of screens.
- If a field is only valid for a few projects or issue types, then limit its scope with a custom field context.

Where Is My Field?

With all of the different ways to hide fields in JIRA, JIRA administrators are commonly asked "Where is my field?". This may seem like an opportunity to show off your prowess at differentiating between screens, field configurations, and contexts, but resist the urge to invoke your inner Sherlock Holmes. JIRA has a feature exactly for this question and you'll save yourself a tremendous amount of time by using it. This feature is appropriately named "Where is my field?" and is documented at *https://confluence.atlassian.com/display/JIRA/JIRA+Admin +Helper#JIRAAdminHelper-PermissionHelper*.

The "Where is my field?" feature (Figure 6-5) is available to administrators on any issue's create, edit, or view screen, and also via the Configure Fields button. It is excellent for quickly assessing the reason that a field is absent in that particular scenario. In addition to determining if a field has been left off a screen, is hidden by a field configuration, or is excluded from a context, it can also detect whether a field is missing from the view screen simply because its value has not been set.

> Custom fields with empty values do not appear on the view screen. This is a common cause of user confusion, but does save space on the screen.

One scenario that the "Where is my field?" feature will not detect is when a field has been hidden by the create or edit screen's Configure Fields option. This option allows the user to select which optional fields are displayed on a screen and is intended to allow people to streamline their create screens. It's not uncommon for users and administrators alike to forget they have hidden fields this way.

If you have gone through all of the above checks and the field is still missing, then you have my permission to get out your tweed and your pipe, call up Watson, and set about investigating. You have a case to crack! At this point you should probably check what add-ons are installed and whether any custom JavaScript code has been embedded in the field description in your field configuration.

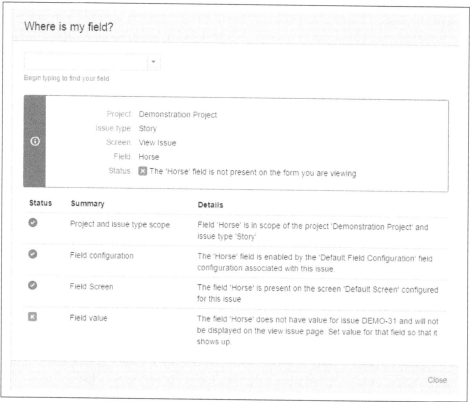

Figure 6-5. In this case the Horse field does not appear on the View Issue screen because it has no value. Note that "Project and issue type scope" refers to the field's context.

Minimizing the Number of Custom Fields

This chapter started off by stressing the importance of minimizing the number of custom fields use in JIRA. This section presents several strategies that can be used to do that. The section after this one describes how to correct the problem of already having too many custom fields.

Use generic field names

Making your custom field names generic enough to be reused for different purposes is critical for minimizing the number of custom fields. Several other strategies discussed here assume that you have used a generic name to begin with. The primary idea here is that you are more likely to be able to reuse an existing field rather than create a new one if you have used generic names for your fields. For example, a field named "Document Link" can be applied more widely than one named "Link to Insurance Form."

Use a new context instead of a new custom field

For any new custom field request, you should check to see if an existing field will fit the need. All that is required is that the field have an appropriate name and be of the correct field type. Remember that option field values can be made completely different for each JIRA project using custom field contexts.

Add field details using a description in a field configuration

Your users may be disappointed with generic field names. In this case, the best strategy to appease them is to add detailed information about the field using a field configuration. Field descriptions in field configurations override the original custom field's description and give you the opportunity to impress the details of the field that are lost through the use of a generic name. To use the "Document Link" field example from earlier, if the intention of this field is to hold a link to a specific type of document then it is good practice to add a helpful description (such as "Provide a link to your Insurance Form") to the field description in the relevant field configuration.

Rely heavily upon the Description system field

Multiline text fields are exceptional for catching a lot of information in a single field. However, the Description system field that comes with JIRA is typically sufficient. If the purpose of a proposed multiline text field is to simply contain more information about the issue, the prudent thing to do is to simply roll that functionality into the Description field.

Use the default value for multiline text fields to create templates

One argument in favor of using custom multiline text fields is that they can be given default values, whereas system text fields like Description cannot. This allows you to create a template by embedding the template as the default value for the field. For example, a good bug report will contain the steps to reproduce the bug, the actual result, and the expected result. Rather than create three separate fields, you can create one multiline text field with three headers ("Steps to Reproduce," "Actual Result," and "Expected Result") in the default value.

Don't try to recreate long surveys in JIRA

Surveys and questionnaires often have long lists of what may appear to be custom fields. Creating a custom field for each question for a short, generic survey is fine, but naming a field something like "Describe your biggest concern about the new coffee machine" is not very reusable. Adding thirty custom fields for a single survey has too great of an impact on the instance as a whole to justify using custom fields for survey questions.

Use JIRA links instead of URL fields

Unless your URL link is intended to be a required field, use the link operation to add web links to an issue, rather than capturing that information in a URL field.

Challenge all requests for new fields
> When I administer a JIRA instance, I require a meeting with every user who requests a new custom field. This allows me to interpret their requirements for the field and explain why I am such a stickler about adding new fields. Cooperative requesters will then work with you to figure out if an existing field can be repurposed or if the field is needed at all. Do not be overly stingy though. If a user has a valid request for a new field, give it to them, because that's what custom fields were made for.

Verify that each field has a purpose
> Ensure that the information captured by each field serves a justifiable purpose. If the data is not used to work on the issue, or for reporting, then it is not needed. It's worth checking with a JQL query how custom fields are actually being used on a quarterly basis.

Establish and share a governance policy
> Create a clear and definitive set of regulations that establish how new objects such as custom fields and configurations are added to JIRA. A governance policy conveys that you have a well–thought-out plan with regard to how JIRA is managed. It is also much more difficult to argue with a document than with a person.

Get executive backing
> You can exercise every bit of advice listed above but it will all be for naught if you can't enforce it. Share your governance policy with relevant managers and executives at your organization and impress upon them your need for their support in keeping JIRA running smoothly. Be ready to substantiate your policy with facts.

Reducing the Number of Custom Fields

Controlling the number of custom fields proactively is one thing, but what if you already have more than a few hundred custom fields in your instance? The truth is that there is no easy path to reducing the number of custom fields once they are already in place and in use. It is a time-consuming process and requires that a great deal of care be taken to ensure that no critical data is lost. But if you are already experiencing significant performance issues due to more than around 600 custom fields, this is still an efficient way to improve performance.

To start with, you should be looking for fields that are used so rarely that they need not exist, or fields that could potentially be merged with another field. To determine how widely a field is used, the Issue Statistics gadget on a JIRA dashboard can prove very useful. Edit the gadget and group by the custom field in question. Then little-used fields will either have very few non-empty values or very few non-default values. Your saved filter can also order by the Updated system field to see when an issue with a value in the field was last updated. If it was more than a year ago, then maybe that field is no longer being used?

 Be careful if your instance has projects that have restricted the browse permission. If you are unable to view a project's issues as a JIRA administrator, then their data won't contribute to your searches or gadgets, and you will get inaccurate results. To further complicate matters, your instance may also be using issue security schemes that restrict the visibility of specific issues. Resolving these obstacles will depend on the specifics of your instance. Just ensure you do not accidentally expose any data to the wrong users in the process.

One way to find candidates for merging fields is to create a list of fields for each custom field type in a spreadsheet outside of JIRA. This process will initially be tedious (the REST resource `rest/api/latest/field.json` may help) but will pay dividends as you can limit your scope for matches to only the relevant field type. This will also give you a place to make notes about which fields to merge after you contact the relevant JIRA project leads.

Merging fields can be dangerous. Make sure you document your process well and are cautious to not lose data. You also need to announce these changes to your users so that they can update any filters, dashboards, and agile boards as needed after the merge.

The most important step of all is to implement policies to control custom field growth after you have completed your field reduction.

Dos and Don'ts

This summary section contains some tips about managing custom fields that did not fit into any of the earlier sections, and some that bear repeating. The tips are included here as a list of Dos and Don'ts.

Dos

- Reuse existing fields when possible.
- Make field names as generic as possible.
- Give your custom fields useful descriptions, including examples of valid field values.
- Mind the formatting of your custom field names. Uncapitalized fields are inconsistent with JIRA's defaults, and even if you do not find them ugly, someone else will.

- Be careful of trailing spaces or other non-visible characters added to custom field names. This will make using scripts harder.
- Err on the side of flexibility. For example, a multiselect field is more flexible than a single-select field, and choosing one might keep you from painting yourself into a corner down the road.
- Translate custom field names for your users who are using a different language pack.
- Know how and when to use custom field contexts.
- Use the "Where is my field?" feature to track down missing fields.
- Have an accessible governance policy in place to express your management strategy to your users.
- Minimize the number of screen and field configuration schemes in JIRA by using screens, field configurations, and custom field contexts appropriately.

Don'ts

- Don't create custom fields with duplicate names. This generally leads to unforeseen problems with reporting, add-ons, custom scripts that refer to fields by name, and other administrative mistakes.
- Don't get around the above tip by using punctuation or different letter case. If you absolutely need to have two fields with similar names, use a thesaurus or append something to the field name to make the distinction clear. Language is a beautiful and varied thing.
- Don't name a field something bizarre like a single space. Just because JIRA lets you do something doesn't mean it won't break JIRA somewhere.
- Don't use whole numbers for option field values. This tip applies mostly to the system fields Status, Resolution, and especially Priority. The trouble here is that in a JQL search, JIRA is happy to find value IDs right alongside actual string values. To complicate matters, JIRA's defaults for each of these fields come with single-digit IDs. If you have a Priority level whose name is "4" and whose ID is 3, it will show up in both a search for `priority = 3` and `priority = 4`, leading to confused users and administrators.
- Don't create option fields that have to be updated frequently. For example, a select list with usernames will quickly become outdated as people's roles change. For a busy administrator, such a list is unmaintainable. Field options should be at least semi-permanent.
- Don't add the option value *None*. This option already exists when the field is made optional and adding it to the list makes reporting harder.

- Don't count on Label field values to be consistent.
- Don't lose data. Remember that fields are where the data lives and editing those field should call for a related amount of caution. Deleting a custom field means that the data is gone—JIRA has no Undo feature.

CHAPTER 7

The User Lifecycle

Overview

One of the areas that a new JIRA administrator commonly feels uncertain about is adding, modifying, and deactivating users in JIRA. This chapter covers some of the different aspects of the lifecycle of a JIRA user.

Adding Users

Before someone can log into JIRA, a JIRA administrator has to create a user account for them. A JIRA administrator is someone in the jira-administrators or jira-system-administrators groups,[1] not someone in the project role *Administrators*.

As one might expect, JIRA has an internal user directory of user accounts, but there are also a number of other ways to define JIRA users.

When you add new users to JIRA you can just look an existing user's groups and take those as a template for what the new user needs. However this can soon become confusing. A better idea is to have the expected use of JIRA groups and project roles documented somewhere for each JIRA project. It's an odd quirk that JIRA groups don't have a description associated with them, and cannot be easily renamed.

The most common request is to have JIRA work with user accounts that have already been defined for other applications and network domains. For example, many organ-

---

[1] The differences between these two groups are described at *http://confluence.atlassian.com/display/JIRA/ Managing+Global+Permissions#ManagingGlobalPermissions-sysadmin*. Broadly speaking a JIRA administrator can make changes that don't affect how JIRA interacts with the local filesystem, OS or other systems, and a system administer can do everything.

izations have a Microsoft Active Directory (AD) server where users and groups are defined. Such groups may even contain email aliases that users can modify themselves. JIRA can use such directory services in a number of different ways:

Authentication
> The passwords for JIRA users are the same as their passwords in the external directory service. This is usually the easiest one to set up.

Authorization
> The different groups that JIRA users belong to are defined in the directory service. This often means that changes to group membership have to be performed by the directory service administrators.

Provisioning of User Accounts
> The user accounts in JIRA are automatically created when they appear in the directory service. Automatic deactivation of accounts requires that the groups are also defined in the directory service.

Atlassian has a directory service product named Crowd (*http://www.atlassian.com/software/crowd*) that integrates with JIRA and all the other Atlassian products such as Confluence, FishEye/Crucible and Bamboo. This allows you to manage all your Atlassian users and their groups in one place. Crowd can synchronize its list of users from another directory service such as AD or Google Apps.

However, as of JIRA 4.3, much of the user management aspect of Crowd was merged into JIRA, where a "user directory" can be defined for each external directory service. Crowd is still required for single sign-on (SSO) or possibly large numbers of users. However I have used JIRA alone with 15,000 users directly with no problems.

 Even if you are just evaluating JIRA, make sure you use the same userids in JIRA as your local IT team has already used. Changing a JIRA userid later on to match the one used in LDAP is annoyingly difficult prior to JIRA 6.0. And don't ever create a user named "unassigned"!

For more detailed information about the different ways to add users to JIRA and user directories, please see the documentation at *http://confluence.atlassian.com/display/JIRA/Managing+Users* and *http://confluence.atlassian.com/display/JIRA/Configuring+User+Directories*.

Adding Third-Party Users

A common requirement is to give a group of third-party users, such as contractors, access to only some of JIRA. One way to do that is as follows:

1. Create a new JIRA group named something like "third-party-users." Add the third-party users to this group, but do *not* add them to the default jira-users group that all your staff are in.

2. At the Global permissions page (Administration→System→Global permissions), grant the *JIRA Users* permission to the new third-party-users group. This will allow the members of that group to log into JIRA.

3. Now go to each JIRA project where you want the third-party users to be able to view or edit issues. Add the new third-party-users group to the appropriate project roles. This is usually the Users or Developers role, but depends on the local permission scheme used by the project.

JIRA restricts who can see user names and email addresses according to the groups that have the global permission "Browse Users." However, there are a few obscure ways in which this data can leak out.

Be careful when using permissions such as "Any Users" or "All Users." In JIRA, this generally allows *anonymous* access to JIRA, where a user can view or edit issues without logging in. This is not usually what was intended. Also, giving the Reporter the "Browse Projects" permission in a permission scheme allows all JIRA users to view that project. Use an issue security scheme instead.

Modifying Users

The only constant is change, so you should expect JIRA user accounts to need updating. If a user is defined in the JIRA internal user directory, then changing a user's email address and full name is easy enough to do: go to Administration→User Management→Users, find the user, and click Edit. If the user is defined in an external LDAP directory (such as Active Directory), you most likely can't change these details from within JIRA. The Directory Configuration Summary link at Administration→User Management→User Directories shows the allowed operations for each user directory. Note that very few AD instances ever allow the applications that use them to change data in AD.

You can't edit the details of a User Directory when you are logged in as a user from that User Directory, so always keep a JIRA system administrator account defined in the internal JIRA directory to make sure you can log in. This is particularly useful if your AD server details need to be changed after refreshing a staging JIRA instance.

JIRA requires that all users created in the JIRA internal user directory have an email address. However users from external user directories can be created without email addresses. This can cause occasional errors to be seen in log files but doesn't seem to have any other effects.

JIRA doesn't check for duplicate email addresses for its users, so you can create two users with the same email address. However, both JIRA users may be sent email from within JIRA, which will result in receiving duplicate emails at the same email address. This is confusing, so avoid using duplicate email addresses when possible. Also, if an email message is used to create a comment on an issue (see the section "Email" on page 95), JIRA assumes that the comment was sent by the first user whose email address matches the *From* address in the email.

As an aside, a user's full name can also be used to contain information about their affiliation (e.g., "John Smith [Example Company]"). The full name can be up to 255 characters.

Changing a Username

A name change after marriage is a common reason for a request to change a JIRA username, sometimes also referred to as the "userid" or "Username." As of JIRA 6.0, this can be changed like any other user detail. However, the old username cannot be reused again later on.

Prior to JIRA 6.0, the full name ("Jane Smith") of the user could be changed easily enough, but changing the username (jane.smith) was much harder to do so cleanly.

If you have simply created a user and made an error entering the username, then deleting the user and starting again can be the best approach. But once a JIRA user is active, then deleting a user is not allowed while there are issues assigned to the user, or reported by the user, or comments by that user. Deleting a active user also removes useful historical information from issues so should be avoided when possible.

Deactivating Users

When a user should no longer have access to JIRA, they can be *deactivated*. This is preferable to *deleting* them, which removes useful historical information (and is also more work in older versions of JIRA). The term is also less ambiguous than *disabling* someone. A deactivated user cannot log in and also does not appear in lists of users (e.g., for assigning issues).

The steps to deactivate a user are simple:

1. Go to Administration→User Management→Users.

2. Find the user, and click Edit.

3. Uncheck the Active checkbox and click Update.

The user will no longer appear be able to log in to JIRA even though they are not removed from the `jira-users` group. The user does not count towards the licensed user count. Their name will have "(Inactive)" appended, and they will not receive email (except for Subscriptions). However, any issues currently assigned to the user will still be assigned to the same inactive user. A bulk change can be used to reassign those issues to an active user. More details can be found at *http://bit.ly/11CYl4W*.

Handling deactivated users in external directory services is more involved. Such users are commonly marked as inactive in AD and then periodically moved to an inactive area by an IT team. If the user is actually deleted from AD, then the best approach is to create users in the JIRA internal user directory, and then deactivate the user as usual. This will preserve the history of the user in JIRA issues. Otherwise JIRA will display "Anonymous" instead of the userid in earlier versions of JIRA. In more recent versions the userid will be displayed, but not as a link. Editing issues with non-existent users can cause errors if the reporter is required.

Users in JIRA Cloud have their access to the different Atlassian applications granted or revoked. This adds or removes the user from specific groups which control what the user can do. You can also deactivate users in JIRA Cloud just as in JIRA Server.

Monitoring Users

An often overlooked feature in JIRA is the ability to see which users are logged in by using Administration→System→User sessions. This feature can be useful during upgrades (see Chapter 8) for checking who needs to log out before the upgrade can begin. You can also send email to such users from within JIRA at Administration→System→Send mail.

If the JIRA users are defined in an external directory service, then it's often helpful to disable the CAPTCHA password protection (navigate to Administration→System→Settings, and clear the Maximum Authentication Attempts Allowed value). This is because if a user has locked themselves out of an Active Directory server with multiple failed password attempts, then entering a correct CAPTCHA will never unlock their password, and so just causes confusion. CAPTCHAs work best when all the users are in the JIRA internal user directory.

CHAPTER 8

Planning a JIRA Upgrade

Overview

Atlassian has released two new versions of JIRA each year for some years now. Recent releases and their dates are listed at *https://confluence.atlassian.com/display/JIRA/ JIRA+Release+Summary* and include:

JIRA 6.0—May 2013
JIRA 6.1—September 2013
JIRA 6.2—February 2014
JIRA 6.3—July 2014
JIRA 6.4—March 2015
JIRA 7.0—End of 2015

Major versions such as 6.3 and 6.4 are supported for "two years after the first release of that version. " For example, JIRA 6.4 was released on March 17th, 2015, so it will be supported by Atlassian until March 17th, 2017. This is a change from an earlier policy that supported versions until two years after their final patch release. The current end-of-life details for JIRA and other Atlassian products are available at *https:// confluence.atlassian.com/display/Support/Atlassian+Support+End+of+Life+Policy*.

All of this means that upgrading JIRA on a yearly basis is a common practice. The process of upgrading JIRA is complex enough to warrant having a chapter dedicated to it, especially since doing it once per year is just long enough to mislay your notes from the last time you did the same job. The Atlassian documentation about upgrading JIRA starts at *https://confluence.atlassian.com/display/JIRA/Upgrading+JIRA* and lists a number of different approaches. This chapter describes an upgrade procedure that corresponds most closely to *Upgrading JIRA Manually (https://confluence.atlas sian.com/display/JIRA/Upgrading+JIRA+Manually)* and can be used over and over—

though of course, it also depends on the specific release notes for each JIRA version, which are published at *http://confluence.atlassian.com/display/JIRA/Production+Relea ses*.

Preparing for an Upgrade

The very first thing to do is to work out which JIRA version you're allowed to upgrade to. JIRA licenses permit you to upgrade to any newer version released during a period when you are covered by a support contract. The first year of support comes bundled with the initial purchase. So if you bought JIRA on July 9th, 2014 then you are allowed to upgrade to any version released before July 9th, 2015, which includes JIRA 6.4. However, if the next version (7.0) happens to be released in October 2015, then you'll have to renew your support contract to be able to upgrade to it. You can find your support details at Administration→System→License.

 Upgrading with a license that doesn't cover the new version will stop the process dead, sometimes not cleanly. I recommend only upgrading to versions of JIRA that were released during the period covered by your license's support dates. However, evaluation licenses can be used to test an upgrade on a staging server.

The next thing to do is to make sure that your backups are working. If you don't have a full *Bare Metal Recovery* procedure to test them with, then at least check that recent backups of the data and attachments are being created and contain some reasonable-looking data.

The hardest part of JIRA upgrades used to be working out whether all third-party add-ons were compatible with the new version of JIRA. You had to look up each add-on listed in Administration→Add-ons→Manage add-ons at the Atlassian Marketplace (`marketplace.atlassian.com`, formerly `plugins.atlassian.com`) by hand. If your JIRA instance is behind a firewall and cannot connect to the Marketplace, then you may still have to do this. But most JIRA administrators can now simply use the JIRA Upgrade Check feature at Administration→Add-ons→Manage add-ons to get the same information.

You may ask "what can I do if I'm using an add-on that isn't compatible with the new version of JIRA?" Check if there is already an open issue at wherever that add-on tracks issues about compatibility (the add-on's own issue tracker, not `jira.atlas sian.com`), and create a support request if there isn't one already there. If the add-on is supported, you can also try contacting the add-on vendor. Some add-ons take months after a new JIRA release to catch up, which is one reason why some people choose to wait for the first dot release (i.e., 7.0.1 instead of 7.0).

The upgrade procedure described below assumes that you have a development or staging instance of JIRA, which is one configured just like your production instance and containing a recent snapshot of the data from the production instance—but which is only used by you. If this is not the case and you only have one JIRA instance (which is your production JIRA), then the upgrade job will take a little less time but is more risky, so make doubly sure that your backups are valid.

Many instances of JIRA are integrated with many other applications as well as email and LDAP. There may be scripts that access JIRA remotely to retrieve or modify information for other systems. These integrations should all be tested with an upgraded development JIRA instance before upgrading a production JIRA. You may need to check the JIRA access logs to find out where scripts that regularly access JIRA remotely are coming from.

The amount of effort a JIRA upgrade takes usually corresponds to the number of issues (size of data), the number of add-ons and the number of other systems that are integrated with JIRA.

You may also want to start planning possible dates for the upgrade with your users and other groups. Most upgrades I've done recently seemed to require about two hours of JIRA downtime. However in-place database upgrades (see the section "Upgrade Approaches" on page 86) and improved installers have somewhat reduced this time for large JIRA instances. For large instances of JIRA the upgrade time is nearer to six hours, with most of the time spent on a full reindex.

Important JIRA Locations

There are at least four locations or services involved in every working JIRA instance. These are:

jira_app
> The *JIRA Install* directory; this is where JIRA was unpacked and is named something like *atlassian-jira-core-7.0.0-standalone* or *atlassian-jira-6.4.4-standalone*. On Linux, I usually create a soft link named *jira_app* to the install directory from its parent directory to make future upgrades easier, like this:

```
lrwxr-xr-x jira jira 40 May  7 08:00 \
          jira_app@ -> atlassian-jira-core-7.0.0-standalone
```

jira_data
> The *JIRA Home* directory; this is where JIRA stores any data that isn't in the database. This includes files that are added as attachments to issues, files for add-ons, project avatars, and caches of the database data in the Lucene index files. This is

the directory name that is configured in the *jira-application.properties* file under the install directory.

This directory can be named anything you wish, but I usually name it something like *jira_data_700* if it is being used for a JIRA 7.0.0 installation. On Linux, I usually create a soft link named *jira_data* to the JIRA home directory at the same level. Don't put the JIRA data directory under the install directory or an installer-driven upgrade will not work.

Database

The database used by JIRA contains both the issues added by JIRA users, the JIRA configuration that is changed by JIRA administrators and add-on data. The two major sets of files that are not kept in the database are attachments and add-on jar file, which are kept in *jira_data*. Avatars (custom project icons) are also not in the database.

The database configuration is stored in a file named *dbconfig.xml* in the *jira_data* directory. If you are using the non-production evaluation H2 database, it is stored in the *jira_data/database* directory.

User Directory

User directories are where JIRA keeps its lists of users. By default, JIRA uses an internal user directory which is stored in the database. If Active Directory, Crowd, or some other separate directory service is used, then the upgraded JIRA needs to use that too—otherwise no one will be able to log in, including JIRA administrators (see "Adding Users" on page 77). It's always a good idea to keep one user with JIRA system administration rights in the JIRA internal user directory for this reason.

Upgrade Approaches

The upgrade procedure as described in "A General Upgrade Procedure" on page 87 uses a new database for the new instance of JIRA. Leaving the database used by the current JIRA instance untouched makes abandoning an upgrade easy. However, using a new database does mean that the data has to be migrated either by a Database Administrator using a database tool to copy it, or using an XML backup file which can be very large and somewhat slow to generate for large JIRA instances. You may also want to disable auto-export for large JIRA instances as *documented*.

The alternative is to upgrade the database in place. This means that you can reuse the same database for the new instance. The database schema, including the database indexes, will be modified by the new instance of JIRA when it starts up. Of course, you should back up at the database level before that occurs, and upgrading a development JIRA instance first is still a good idea.

Simple Upgrades

If you aren't changing your machine or database in any way and you're using Linux or Windows, then you can simply follow the steps listed at *https://confluence.atlas sian.com/display/JIRA/Upgrading+JIRA+Using+a+Rapid+Upgrade+Method* and download the appropriate installer.

The installer will prompt you for the necessary information and also save your inputs so you can rerun an upgrade as necessary. One difference is that JIRA is shipped with a Java Runtime Environment (JRE) that it uses by default. Setting the JAVA_HOME environment variable no longer changes which Java VM is used; you have to edit bin/permgen.sh, which is where the installer sets JAVA_HOME.

A General Upgrade Procedure

This section describes a general procedure for upgrades that is applicable to all versions of JIRA and to changing the server, database, or even OS. Since no procedure can fit every upgrade precisely, please use it only as a basis for your own customized upgrade procedure. Briefly, the procedure looks like this:

- Install and configure the new, upgraded JIRA instance ready for data.
- Take an XML backup of the current JIRA instance and shut it down.
- Import the XML backup into the upgraded JIRA instance and test it.
- Declare the upgrade complete.

These steps are similar to the ones in the documentation at *http://confluence.atlassian.com/display/JIRA/Upgrading+JIRA+Manually*.

The four instances of JIRA referred to in this upgrade procedure are:

- The current production JIRA (e.g., version 6.2)
- The upgraded production JIRA (e.g., version 7.0), usually on the same server as the current production JIRA—upgrading JIRA and moving JIRA to a new server are two steps that are best done separately
- The current development JIRA (e.g., version 6.2)
- The upgraded development JIRA (e.g., version 7.0), often on the same server as the current development JIRA

If you don't have a development instance of JIRA, then your production instance is effectively your development instance, and your upgrade is done after Step 15.

The upgrade steps follow:

1. As usual before changing anything, create a backup. Then start taking your own notes about each of the upcoming steps. Record what you did and any unexpected results.

2. Unpack the new version of JIRA on the development server, making sure the files are owned by the service account that will run JIRA. This location is the new *jira_app* directory for this instance. Any existing *jira_app* soft link will eventually refer to this directory when the upgrade is complete.

3. Create a new JIRA Home directory named *jira_data_70* for the new development JIRA instance. Any existing *jira_data* soft link will eventually refer to this directory.

4. Create a new, empty database for the new development JIRA instance. Make sure that the database uses the correct character set, collation order, table type, and so forth (or at least the same ones as the existing JIRA database).

5. Configure the new development JIRA files. Some of the files in *jira_app* that are likely to be changed include:

   atlassian-jira/WEB-INF/classes/jira-application.properties
   Used to set *jira.home* to the absolute path of *jira_data*.

   bin/setenv.sh
   Used to change the JVM memory settings and to uncomment DISABLE_NOTIFICATIONS so that the development instance doesn't send or retrieve email. Note that you can still use the "Send a Test Email" feature even with the rest of email disabled. JIRA on Windows uses the Registry to store the JVM settings when running as a service.

   lib/*.jar
   You should check that the JDBC driver jar file for your database is available here. Recent versions of JIRA ship with the drivers for PostgreSQL and Oracle but not MySQL.

6. If the current JIRA has a *jira_data/jira-config.properties* file, then make sure this is copied over to the new JIRA. This file contains advanced configuration changes that can't be made in the UI, as documented at *https://confluence.atlassian.com/display/JIRA/Advanced+JIRA+Configuration*. If no such changes have been made, then this file will not exist.

Copy or modify any other files such as custom icons for issue types, priorities, resolutions and statuses, or a logo image file. You can find a list of files that have been changed in the current production JIRA under Administration→System→System info, Modifications. If you added any custom event templates (see the section "Workflows and Events" on page 53) or changed your email templates, you'll also need to merge them over to the upgraded instance.

 It's about now that I usually start to wish I had used version control or a tool such as *puppet* or *chef* to record the changes I made to the current JIRA when I last upgraded it. It's not too late to start!.

7. If you want to, you can install any updated add-on files that you've downloaded manually at this stage. Having the add-ons in place will reduce the number of error log messages about missing add-ons when you import data into the new instance.

    Add-on *.jar* files go in *jira_data/plugins/installed-plugins* (you'll have to create this directory). If an add-on's installation involves more than just copying a *.jar* file, I usually postpone installing it until after this step. Some add-ons use *.obr* files that have to be uploaded not preinstalled (these are bundles of *.jar* files).

8. Export the data from the current production instance as a compressed XML backup file (Administration→System→Backup system). Use a filename that includes the JIRA version, date and time. If your JIRA instance is too large for this, then use a copy of the production database.

    There is a short period here where JIRA is still active but an XML backup is running. Any changes made by users during this period will be lost when the upgrade is complete, so make sure you warn people not to use JIRA after a certain time.

    You may ask "Why can't I just make my current JIRA read-only?" You could do this, but then the port used by JIRA is still in use, and the new instance can't use it. Also, there's no really convenient way to allow users to log in to a read-only instance, which is necessary for issue security.

9. Make sure any automated script and network monitoring systems are aware of the upcoming outage and then shut down the production JIRA instance. This is when the clock starts timing for just how long the upgrade inconveniences your JIRA users.

10. Create a new directory called *jira_data/data/import* in the new development instance.

11. Copy the XML backup file into the *import* directory, or create a soft link to it there.

12. Start up the new JIRA development instance and browse to the start page. You shouldn't be prompted to log in since you're using a new database and a new *jira_data* directory. Choose the option to let you set up JIRA yourself, not the option for a demonstration instance.

 If you are prompted to log in then you've probably just done an in-place database upgrade (see the section "Upgrade Approaches" on page 86) and you can skip the next step of importing the XML backup. However, if you stop the upgrade after this point, you will need to restore the database from a database backup.

13. Click on the link to import your existing data and give the name of the XML backup file in the import directory. Disable outgoing mail if given the choice. Then click *Restore*.

If you need to update the license for this version of JIRA, you will be prompted for a new license key.

You may also get a message about an import failing because the paths for the index directory or attachments directory wasn't found. This means that these directories were at locations in the current JIRA instance that don't exist on the upgraded instance. In that case, just click the "retry with default paths" link.

You can follow the progress of the import in *jira_app/logs/catalina.out* or in *jira_data/log/atlassian-jira.log*. It may take some minutes to parse the XML, store the generic entities to the new database, create the Lucene indexes, apply database schema changes, and reindex for each schema change. The longest part of all this is usually the reindexing for every schema change and can take some hours for large instances.

14. Copy the attachments over to the new *jira_data/data/attachments* directory. This can also take some time if there are many large attachments. Check for other directories with any content in *jira_data/data* and copy them too.

15. Once JIRA is available again, you will want to test it as described in the next section, "Testing an Upgrade" on page 91.

16. After giving users some time to test the upgraded development instance, repeat all these steps for the production JIRA instance.

You can set a banner across the top of all of JIRA's pages using Administration→System→Announcement banner. This is a great way to warn users of an upcoming JIRA outage. For extra notice, you can use the existing CSS by surrounding your banner text with div elements:

```
<div class="infoBox">
Your announcement text goes here.
</div>
```

but be careful since invalid HTML here can make JIRA unusable until you clear it in the database (*https://confluence.atlas sian.com/display/JIRAKB/How+to+remove+JIRA +Announcement+Banner+through+the+database*).

17. After the upgrade, you will need to change the name of the database that should be backed up. You may also need to change the JIRA Home directory location in the backup scripts. Any startup scripts to start JIRA after a server reboot should be checked too. If you have used soft links for *jira_data* and *jira_app*, then fewer things should have to change.

    Update any local Bare Metal Recovery documents and other administration notes, take a breath, and you're done!

Testing an Upgrade

The first and easiest test is whether user authentication is working—can you log in?

Start at the Administration→System→System info page and look for errors or outdated settings. Does the Base URL need to change? Do the locations for Attachments, Indexing, and the Backup Service at Administration→Services look correct?

If the upgraded JIRA is a development instance, then you can compare it to the production JIRA directly in a browser. Compare the Administration→System→System info pages for unexpected differences. Pick three issues at random and check that their data, including some attachments, is the same. You can also print all this out to use when testing the production JIRA after it is upgraded. Remember that some filter results will look different if they have any kind of date clause in them.

The most likely area for trouble with an upgrade is with third-party add-ons. Check the list of add-ons for disabled add-ons or individual add-on modules.

Check that all the known integrations of other applications with JIRA are working as expected. Check that the scripts that access JIRA remotely are also still working.

Another useful test is to count the number of custom fields in the development instance and in the production instance. Disabled custom field from add-ons may be responsible for any difference in numbers.

Check that all the custom fields that used to be searchable in the Issue Navigator are still searchable. If not, then a custom field searcher add-on may not be working.

If the upgraded JIRA is the production JIRA, then check that attachments can be downloaded from issues and that email can be sent and received.

The most likely place to notice that something is wrong is in the directory *jira_app/ logs/catalina.out*. Searching in this file for ERROR and WARN will usually suggest things to investigate further. To me, a good upgrade is one that results in a minimal number of such warning messages in log files, and no log messages that repeat every minute and cause the log file to become bloated. I also like the Log Scanner, available at Administration→System→Atlassian support tools, which checks the JIRA log for known issues using text patterns. It does raise some false positives, but can be useful for a preliminary error check and provides links to the appropriate JIRA Knowledge Base articles for each error.

Troubleshooting an Upgrade

Most JIRA upgrades go just fine, but sometimes what was intended to be just a quick upgrade turns into a Bad Day. You've got frustrated users and only a few cryptic error messages to go on. What now?

If this is the upgraded production instance, then you should probably abandon the upgrade and let people use the current production JIRA instance again. To do that, simply stop the upgraded instance of JIRA, change any soft links back to where they used to point, and restart the current instance of JIRA.

Then check whether it was really a problem at all. Some messages in JIRA log files can appear alarming, but aren't in fact all that serious. For example, if you haven't installed an add-on that provides a custom field type then you will see an error like:

```
2011-04-16 21:54:23,847 main ERROR [jira.issue.managers.
    DefaultCustomFieldManager] Could not load custom field type plugin with
    key ... Is the plugin present and enabled?
```

JIRA preserves the data in any custom fields that use such custom field types, but doesn't display the custom field at Administration→Issues→Custom fields. This means that you can't delete such fields and that you will see the error message every time you restart JIRA. Old services and listeners can generate similar error messages in log files.

More troublesome are messages that keep occurring, filling up a log file and making it harder to use when real problems occur. These are always worth tracking down—or as a last resort, reducing the log level for just that area in *log4j.properties*.

Other approaches to use when troubleshooting an upgrade are:

- Log into JIRA using the simplest URL possible. If you have forwarding set up with Apache or NGINX, then disable that temporarily and use the default JIRA URL with `http` and port 8080.

- If you can't authenticate using Active Directory, then try logging in as some user that is defined in JIRA's internal directory service. The original JIRA administrator account may even still work for you.

- Check your `https` settings very carefully and only apply them after checking that everything else is working.

If all else fails, contact *Atlassian Support* or an *Atlassian Expert* to ask for help.

Further Reading

The official Atlassian support policy for JIRA can be found at *http://confluence.atlassian.com/display/Support/Atlassian+Support+End+of+Life+Policy*.

Logging in JIRA is configured at Administration→System→Logging and profiling. More detailed documentation about the underlying `log4j` logging framework can be found at *http://logging.apache.org/log4j/1.2/manual.html*.

There is an existing Suggestion to be able to make JIRA read-only at *http://jira.atlassian.com/browse/JRA-1924*.

CHAPTER 9

Remote Access to JIRA

Overview

"No man is an island," wrote John Donne, and this is doubly true of JIRA and almost every other application you may administer. Users want their data to appear in multiple places, administrators want to manage applications from a single place, and anyone may want to run some scripts to make lots of changes at once.

All of these require remote access to JIRA, where "remote access" is defined loosely as using JIRA without a browser.

This chapter covers a variety of remote access methods for JIRA. The quick summary is that REST is the way that most remote access to JIRA occurs in 2015, with a small amount of SOAP access in older installations. SOAP access was deprecated in JIRA 6.0 and removed in JIRA 7.0.

A good starting place for REST information in the Atlassian documentation is *https://developer.atlassian.com/jiradev/jira-apis/jira-rest-apis*.

Email

Email is one of the simplest ways to use JIRA remotely. Issues can be created and then comments added to them using the standard JIRA mail service and mail handlers. Email is a function commonly already found in many applications.[1] Balanced against the simplicity of email are its limitations:

---

1 *Zawinski's Law*: Every program attempts to expand until it can read mail.

- Email messages have limited structure. Only the *To*, *Cc*, *Subject*, *From* fields and any attachments are easily separated from the email body.

- There's no real guarantee about who most email is from, so authentication is hard.

- Email is asynchronous and unreliable, in the sense that retrying failed messages is slow and limited — so you don't know if your message reached JIRA. You may not even get any feedback about whether a JIRA server is currently active.

Still, it's familiar and convenient and a fair number of JIRA users only interact with JIRA via email (see "Further Reading" on page 102). Some integrations between different systems use email, but it's not really a great idea because of the limitations listed above. In addition, standard JIRA has to have a separate mail handler for each JIRA project where issues are created and this does not scale well when there are many projects involved.

SQL

Accessing the underlying database of a JIRA instance is surprisingly common perhaps because, like email, many applications are already accessing their own database and adding one more database is an obvious approach to try. Most access to JIRA's database is for creating reports using a separate report generating tool.

Reading data from the JIRA database using other systems is usually just fine (and is generally pretty fast) but does have the following strict limitations:

- *Access must be read-only.* This is because JIRA caches many of the values read from its database and it may not update the caches until the next time it is restarted. If the data is changed in JIRA before that happens, then the updated values will be written back to the database, overwriting any changes that you made there.

- You have to carefully control who can view the different tables in the JIRA database. For instance, if some issues have issue security schemes (see "Issue Security Schemes" on page 19) defined so that only certain people can see the issues, the underlying confidential data would end up being visible to the database user running the SQL query. That is, all data in the JIRA database can be viewed by a database user.

- The JIRA database schema is only partially documented (*https://developer.atlas sian.com/jiradev/jira-architecture/database-schema*) because the schema does change between different versions of JIRA. JIRA upgrades handle such changes automatically but Atlassian does not encourage (or support) direct database access. The actual file where the database schema is defined (and not documented) is *atlassian-jira/WEB-INF/classes/entitydefs/entitymodel.xml*.

If you do decide to take this approach, then a somewhat dated place to start is *http://confluence.atlassian.com/display/JIRACOM/Example+SQL+queries+for+JIRA*. This page has many SQL queries that other people have found useful. However, most of them don't have much explanation of why they work the way they do.

REST

The recommended way to access JIRA remotely is REST. REST methods are invoked using a URI, plus arguments passed in after the URI.[2] The resulting data from JIRA is in the JSON format. The returned data usually also contains further URIs to let you drill down into the data. This means that clients can "walk" the data and dynamically discover what is currently available.

A good place to start for information about JIRA and REST are the tutorials at *https://developer.atlassian.com/jiradev/jira-apis/jira-rest-apis/jira-rest-api-tutorials*.

If you want to see an example of what JIRA returns with REST for an issue, browse to *http://jira.atlassian.com/rest/api/latest/issue/JRA-13036.json*. Different browsers will display the resulting JSON data differently. The *Pretty JSON* extension is helpful for Chrome users.

Alternatively, you can use a command line tool such as *curl* or *wget*. Replace userid with your Atlassian username from *https://my.atlassian.com* and secret with your password and try the following:

```
curl -u userid:secret \
   http://jira.atlassian.com/rest/api/latest/issue/JRA-13036.json

wget --user=userid --password=secret \
   http://jira.atlassian.com/rest/api/latest/issue/JRA-13036.json
```

REST access to JIRA is reasonably efficient but requests from the same authenticated user are queued for the same thread so overall access may seem slower sometimes. Updating many issues at once is often only at the rate of a few per second. The performance of many REST requests was improved in JIRA 6.4, particularly searching for issues.

Another excellent way to see what REST resources are available and experiment with them is to install the Atlassian Developer Toolbox (*https://marketplace.atlassian.com/plugins/com.atlassian.devrel.developer-toolbox-plugin*) add-on which includes the *REST API browser* tool. This tool lets you choose a set of resources such as Atlassian

---

2 The more familiar URL (Uniform Resource Locator) is one kind of URI (Uniform Resource Identifier).

JIRA - Plugins - REST Plugin, which is the official REST API for JIRA, and explore them. You can also add data and invoke a resource directly from within the page and see the results there.

JIRA and Python

You can use any language that can make an HTTP call to the REST API, but there is a long history of helpful Python libraries for accessing JIRA. The latest in this line is jira-python from *https://github.com/pycontribs/jira/blob/master/README.rst*. This library was originally written by Ben Speakmon but is now maintained by Sorin Sbâr-nea and others. This library can be used as a standalone CLI for accessing JIRA but is more commonly used as a library in a Python script. The short script below shows how it can be used to query JIRA and list the keys of the issues that are returned from the query:

```
from jira.client import import JIRA

# Note the tuple
jira = JIRA(options={'server': 'http://jira.example.com'},
            basic_auth=('jsmith', 'secret'))

# Get the open issues in the TEST project
jql = 'project = TEST and status != Closed'

issues = jira.search_issues(jql)
for issue in issues:
    print issue.key
```

Creating Custom REST Resources

The process of creating your own REST resources by writing a custom JIRA add-on is described at the Atlassian Developers website (*https://developer.atlassian.com/display/DOCS/Developing+a+REST+Service+Plugin*).

If you have to use a compiled language such as Java or C++ for your client, try first using a dynamic language such as Python to create a small test script to prove that any problem is not in the URL, authentication, or the values passed to the resource. This can greatly reduce the time taken for each development iteration.

One example of a custom REST resource is the *Inquisitor Plugin for JIRA* by Sorin Sbârnea (Citrix) available at *https://marketplace.atlassian.com/plugins/com.citrix.jira.inquisitor*. This add-on lets you download the standard JIRA fields for thousands of JIRA issues in a few seconds. Custom fields are not retrieved however. The source code at *https://github.com/ssbarnea/inquisitor* is a useful example of creating your own REST resource.

The History of JIRA and REST

Before JIRA 5, the JIRA REST API could retrieve data, but could not update data. After JIRA 5, issues could be searched for, modified and so on. However, general purpose REST resources for administering JIRA still don't exist.

Since version 4.0, JIRA has been changing internally to use REST for retrieving more of the information that is destined for the UI. The JIRA Dashboard gadgets all use an (undocumented) REST API, as do the Labels and Versions system fields and all the project administration pages. This is all part of the general move in web applications toward Dynamic HTML (DHTML), where JavaScript running in the client's browser asynchronously populates the HTML and CSS that is used to produce the displayed web page. It's also why using a modern browser will make JIRA faster because more work is done in the browser rather than the server.

Webhooks

As discussed in "Workflows and Events" on page 53, JIRA sends internal "events" when issues are changed. Webhooks can be configured in JIRA at Administration→System→WebHooks and also in workflow post functions. When a standard event such as *Issue Created* is sent within JIRA, a webhook can make an HTTP POST call to a remote system. Custom events are not supported but many other events are supported now, making webhooks a useful method to get JIRA to connect to remote systems.

The main Atlassian documentation for webhooks can be found at *https://conflu ence.atlassian.com/display/JIRA/Managing+Webhooks* and includes some other restrictions on what webhooks can do. A very useful page with examples of what the POST data looks like is *https://developer.atlassian.com/jiradev/jira-architecture/ webhooks*. Webhooks are implemented by JIRA listeners though this is not visible to administrators.

XML and RSS

Retrieving an XML file with the details of just one issue is easy with a URL such as *http://jira.atlassian.com/si/jira.issueviews:issue-xml/JRA-13036/JRA-13036.xml*. The XML that's returned is formatted as an RSS feed item, but since it is structured data, it can be processed by clients for integrating other systems with JIRA.

You can also retrieve the results of a search as an XML file using the link under the Export menu in the Issues→Search for issues screen (also known as the Issue Navigator screen). The XML link is the same one that is used for integrating JIRA with Confluence. JIRA provides similar RSS feeds for the activity of individual users and projects as well. Following a JIRA project's activities with an RSS reader application is more efficient than reading email in some ways.

Authentication is probably the hardest part of using RSS feeds for integration. A username and password can be passed in the URL or a user can be prompted for a password, but neither method is particularly robust.

More information can be found in the documentation at *http://confluence.atlassian.com/display/JIRA/Displaying+Search+Results+in+XML*.

CLI (Command Line Interface)

You may just want is a way to interact with JIRA from a command line or with a shell script. For example, you might want to have an automated build system add a new version in JIRA when a new release occurs. Or you might want to make it easier for an IT team to create new internal users in JIRA by providing a small script for them to run.

The main CLI available for JIRA is *JIRA CLI*, a commercial add-on by Bob Swift, now part of Appfire (*https://marketplace.atlassian.com/plugins/org.swift.jira.cli*). This is written entirely in Java, can be invoked from a shell script, and is part of a suite of CLI tools for all of the Atlassian products. Bob's CLI is well-maintained and very well-tested. It uses both REST and direct HTML access internally, but this is unseen by the user.

The `jira-python` library mentioned in "REST" on page 97 also provides a `jirashell` interactive shell for examining data from JIRA

Remote Issue Links

Remote Issue Links make linking JIRA issues to the URLs of objects in other systems much easier. They can also be used to create links to JIRA issues on another JIRA system. The choices are seen by a user when adding a link to a JIRA issue, but remote issue links can also be created and updated using the REST API (*https://developer.atlassian.com/display/jiradev/Guide+-+JIRA+Remote+Issue+Links*).

There is also the unsupported JIRA to JIRA Issue Copy add-on (*https://marketplace.atlassian.com/plugins/com.atlassian.cpji.cpji-jira-plugin*) from Atlassian, which allows users to copy JIRA issues from one JIRA server to another.

Issue Collectors

Up until a few years ago JIRA supported creating issues and other actions using a fixed URL (*https://confluence.atlassian.com/display/JIRA051/Creating+Issues+via+direct+HTML+links*). This was convenient for embedding a "Report a Bug" link in web pages to create JIRA issues in a specific JIRA project. However it was never easy to authenticate the reporter so as of JIRA 5.2 this approach is deprecated. As of JIRA 6.4 it still works for presetting the project and issue type only.

The alternative is Issue Collectors (*https://confluence.atlassian.com/display/JIRA/ Using+the+Issue+Collector*). These are little snippets of JavaScript automatically generated for each project and issue type. These snippets can be added to a web page to provide a form where details for a new issue can be entered. There is also an administration page that shows which issue collectors have recently been used to create issues.

Basic issue collectors are relatively straight-forward to configure and use. Setting default field values and some other customizations are possible using more customized JavaScript as described in the Advanced Use of the JIRA Issue Collector (*https:// confluence.atlassian.com/jira/advanced-use-of-the-jira-issue- collector-296092376.html*) documentation.

Integrating with Other Applications

Whichever method is used for integrating other applications with JIRA, there are a few things are that worth bearing in mind.

Networking outages will inevitably occur and so your integration has to survive them without inconsistent or corrupted data. This means that any synchronous approach such as REST has to be able to retry later on or warn users that something went wrong. Other than changing issues, most JIRA operations are not strictly transactional, which makes integrations harder.

JIRA provides *services*, custom tasks that are periodically executed as frequently as once per minute. This is one way to have an integration be able to recover from errors. Such services may also run when JIRA is started, which could mean a large load on another system if JIRA has been down for a while. In this case, limiting the amount of work that is done in a single run of the service can help.

Synchronizing two systems in only one direction is much simpler than doing it in both directions. If you really do have to do it in both directions, consider very carefully how you're going to avoid infinite loops and which application will maintain the synchronization state (don't try storing it in both). JIRA issues have an Updated date field that can help with that if the systems' clocks are synchronized. You can also use the internal records of everything that has changed.

There is a useful book titled *Enterprise Integration Patterns*, by Gregor Hohpe and Bobby Woolf (Addison-Wesley) that covers these kinds of issues. And if you haven't already read it, then *The Twelve Networking Truths* [RFC 1925 (*http://www.faqs.org/*

rfcs/rfc1925.html)] is brief and applies to many integrations just as well as it does to networking design.

Further Reading

The process of using JIRA via email is documented at *http://confluence.atlassian.com/display/JIRA/Creating+Issues+and+Comments+from+Email*. The most commonly used add-on to do more with this is The Plugin People and Andy Brook's *Enterprise Mail Handler for JIRA* (JEMH). This commercial add-on has an amazing number of features and is well maintained.

The main page for information about the JIRA database schema is *https://developer.atlassian.com/jiradev/jira-architecture/database-schema*. Enabling logging of all SQL queries is described at *https://developer.atlassian.com/display/jiradev/Logging+JIRA+SQL+Queries*.

One good place to look for more general information about REST is *http://en.wikipedia.org/wiki/REST*. More information about JSON and an example of what that format looks like can be found at *http://en.wikipedia.org/wiki/JSON*.

Finally, the whole of the quote from John Donne:

> No man is an Iland, intire of it selfe; every man is a peece of the Continent, a part of the maine; if a Clod bee washed away by the Sea, Europe is the lesse, as well as if a Promontorie were, as well as if a Mannor of thy friends or of thine owne were; any mans death diminishes me, because I am involved in Mankinde; And therefore never send to know for whom the bell tolls; It tolls for thee.
>
> —Devotion XVII (Meditation XVII),
> John Donne, 1624

CHAPTER 10

Migrating Data into JIRA

Overview

This chapter describes how data is migrated into JIRA from other systems, along with suggestions for how to estimate the effort involved in a migration. The short answer is "more than is usually expected."

The "source system" is the system where the data currently is (e.g., Bugzilla, Rally, or even another instance of JIRA). The words "migration" and "import" tend to be used interchangeably. If there is a difference, JIRA has "import" tools, but the whole process is called a "migration." A "merge" is just a migration that leaves existing data unchanged.

 New JIRA administrators sometimes ask "Can I synchronize the source system and JIRA, so I don't have to do a single large export and import?" Synchronization is a lot more work since it has to handle configurations in both systems changing over time. Instead, I recommend migrating the data once and then making the source system available in a read-only mode for a period after the migration to make testing easier. It's also an incentive to move everyone onto a single system together.

Migrating Data from JIRA to JIRA

JIRA comes with the ability to import a JIRA project from a complete XML backup of a difference JIRA instance. This feature can be found at Administration→System→Project import. However as the feature's documentation at *https://conflu ence.atlassian.com/display/JIRA/Restoring+a+Project+from+Backup* says, "restoring a project from a backup is not a trivial task."

The problem is that the target JIRA has to be configured almost *identically* to the source JIRA for the project import to work. This includes custom field names and types, schemes, workflows, and users. The versions of JIRA and most of the add-ons must be identical, too. Getting the configuration right can take multiple attempts for each project import.

However, the biggest problem is that project imports do not include any data from the Active Objects tables in the JIRA database. These tables where complex add-ons such as JIRA Agile, JIRA Service Desk, and others store their data. The end result is that agile boards, sprints, rank, service desks, and test cases and result are all not imported when doing a project import. Project imports also don't import Remote Links or Web Links.

If you are just trying to move some issues from a development JIRA to staging then this approach is worth considering. In general, though, it doesn't do what is needed for most migrations.

Migration Steps

Any migration can be broken down into three main steps: extract, modify, and import.

Extract the Data

Some way to access the data in the source system is needed. This might be a database connection (a local database is fastest), or perhaps a REST or SOAP (Webservices) API for remote systems. The data could even be extracted as a CSV or XML file. Different source systems make it easier or harder to extract the data, and this step can take a long time (often hours).

A common assumption is that it takes one second per issue just to extract the data using REST. Because of how long this takes—and especially if the network access to the source system is intermittent—it's a good idea to save the extracted data locally while developing your migration tools.

Some types of common data in different systems are:

Issue data
> The source issue's summary, description, dates, labels (tags), etc. This is the core information.

Comments
> This is also core information but may be stored separately from the issue data.

Attachments

These are often large enough to take a long time to migrate. JIRA has a 10MB default maximum size per attachment.

Issue History

This is the record of what changes happened when, but is often not preserved because there isn't an easy way to import it into JIRA with the CSV Importer. However the JSON importer can import this information.

Links

This data is about the relationships between source issues. Again, the CSV Importer does not support importing this information but the JSON importer does.

Modify the Data

Once as much of the data has been extracted from the source system as possible (and stored locally), the next step is to modify the data. Almost every field is modified in some way, which is a surprise to many people. This is one of the reasons why CSV exports from the source system often need further changes to work with larger imports.

The kinds of modifications needed include the following:

User ID mapping

For example, a user "john.smith" in the source system needs to be referred to as "jsmith" in JIRA. This can occur when a company has been acquired and its old data is being moved to the new parent company's JIRA. Changing multiple user IDs in JIRA after the import is a lot of work, so such changes are generally done at this stage instead.

Date offsets

The dates in the source system may not be from the same time zone needed for the JIRA instance. They almost certainly won't be in the correct format for importing into JIRA.

Unicode

Some data (such as the summary, description, comments, usernames, and attachment filenames) will likely contain characters that are not UTF-8 encoded, particularly if the text has been cut and pasted from Microsoft applications such as Word or Excel. This data will need to be encoded to be ready for import into JIRA.

Cleaning up dirty data

Over time, most systems accumulate data that doesn't conform to what is currently considered valid data. Some work will likely be needed to handle this data, if only to ignore it.

Merging fields

Some data will not be wanted for JQL queries in JIRA, but still needs to be preserved. This is often done by converting it into a comment. Other fields may be concatenated for use in JIRA.

Splitting a field

Sometimes data in a single field in the source system is split up into multiple fields in JIRA.

Complex mappings

Sometimes the value of a field in JIRA depends on multiple fields in the source system, in a complex way that is better performed by code before the import, rather than manually afterwards.

Import the Data

The most common way to import data into JIRA is to use one to the standard JIRA Importers. There are importers for Bugzilla, Mantis, FogBugz, Pivotal Tracker, Trac, Asana and Redmine, and also for GitHub and Bitbucket. If you can use one of these standard importers then that will always be the fastest and cheapest approach. However, they don't allow for many of the data modifications described in "Modify the Data" on page 105.

There are two standard JIRA Importers that are more general—CSV and JSON. Both of these importers take a file created with the first two steps (extract, modify) and use the data in that file to create issues in JIRA. This approach allows you to import data from many different source systems while still letting you modify the data for customized imports.

I have also used two other approaches in the past. The first was a direct database import using SQL insert commands, which is fast but involves a deeper understanding of the JIRA and add-ons database schemas. The second was a custom add-on in JIRA that extracted data from the source system and creates the issues using JIRA's internal API. This last approach was flexible, but required a local copy of the database to work well for large source systems.

It is also possible to create your own JIRA importer using the tutorial at *https://devel oper.atlassian.com/display/JIRADEV/Tutorial+-+Writing+custom+importer+using +JIRA+importers+plugin*. I'd recommend this approach over modifying the standard JIRA importers, since you can extend and modify them with your own importer.

The JIRA CSV Importer

The CSV import is located at Administration→System→External System Import. Once you have done your first test import, you can save a configuration file to avoid having to re-enter the field mapping again.

During the import the CSV data file is uploaded from your local machine to JIRA via a web page. This can take a long time on a slow connection and could fail due to the default 10 minute timeout. You may also have to increase the maximum attachment size to be able to upload the CSV file.

You can assume a rate of 2 or 3 issues/second for importing the data, depending on how many large attachments are present.

Attachments are referred to in the CSV file either using a `http://` or `file://` URL. If an `http` URL is used, the attachment must be visible in a browser without using any authentication. If a `file` URL is used, then each attachment can be retrieved from the local JIRA `jira_home/import/attachments` directory. The second approach is faster, but either way, the URL has to be encoded as a URL with no invalid characters.

Cloud Differences

Importing data into a JIRA Cloud instance imposes other restrictions on what can be done. If given the choice, I generally prefer JIRA Server for doing migrations rather than JIRA Cloud. The details of the restrictions are described in the following sections.

No Staging Instance

Importing into a Cloud instance is like importing into production. If an import creates unwanted users, they will need to be removed either manually or with an extra script. To delete a test project with more than 5,000 issues, you may need to delete the issues first, typically with a script. One way to work around this is to have another temporary Cloud instance for staging. In this case the user license has to be the same or larger than the production Cloud instance.

Changing CSV Importer Version

The version of the CSV Importer add-on will be updated whenever a new one is available and deployed by Atlassian. This is one more variable to deal with when you're working towards achieving a stable import.

No Attachment Imports with a File URL

You have to use an unauthenticated `http` URL in the CSV file to retrieve attachments. This may not always work as noted at *https://confluence.atlassian.com/display/ CLOUDKB/Importing+Attachments+Into+JIRA+Cloud+Using+CSV*. If contacting Atlassian Support doesn't help, another workaround is to upload the attachments with a script after the import, though this doesn't preserve the attachment author or date.

No Custom Add-ons

You can't create a custom importer add-on and use it with Cloud as you can with a JIRA Server instance.

Estimating a Migration

The three main steps of a migration (extract, modify, import) are repeated many times during development before the final migration, not just once. With large amounts of data, the complete extract and import steps can take hours to run, so it's important to get as much work done with a smaller set of data as possible.

You can assume a rate of one issue/second for extracting the data and a rate of one issue/second for importing the data. Therefore, 36,000 issues will take at least 20 hours to migrate before the users can access the data in JIRA.

Some common tasks in a non-trivial migration and their estimated average duration are shown in Table 10-1. The estimates are averages, and each one can vary substantially, which makes the total effort for a migration quite hard to estimate accurately. The second migration is generally faster than the first one you do.

Table 10-1. Estimated work for a migration

Estimate (Days)	Activity
0.25	Gather information about the source system (type, version, amount of customization done, number of issues)
0.25	Gather information about the target JIRA instance (Server or Cloud, existing custom fields)
0.5	Confirm access to source system as the user sees it, i.e., browser or client application
1	Confirm access to source system as the system level, e.g., database or API
1	Extract the core data for a single issue from the source system
1	Store the extracted data locally
1	Allows restarting of data extraction after network failures if applicable
2	Extract all required data for a single issue from the source system
2	Define mapping from source system to JIRA, particularly for user IDs

Estimate (Days)	Activity
1	Import a single issue's core data into JIRA
1	Import all of a single issue's data into JIRA, including attachments
4	Import all the source system data into JIRA, allowing for multiple iterations
2	Review the imported data
17	**Total number of days**

Most migrations need multiple complete test imports into JIRA, each one with the requested changes at the modification stage or to retrieve updated data from the source system. This makes the whole project take longer than most people expect—that is, weeks, not days.

Further Reading

The main starting documentation page for importing data into JIRA is at *https:// confluence.atlassian.com/display/JIRA/Migrating+from+Other+Issue+Trackers.*

A number of Atlassian Experts offer migration tools for JIRA at *http://bit.ly/114xrmP*, but these are better described as migration services that modify existing migration scripts for each customer. This is because every major migration has its own special needs.

CHAPTER 11

Jiraargh! Frustrations

Overview

I once wrote an article with the provocative title *Bug Trackers: Do They Really All Suck?*. My conclusion was probably not, but that they are all annoying in some way. Why is this? My theory is that it's because tools such as JIRA are used by multiple groups of people. This means that each group has different needs from the same tool, which in turn leads to no one being fully satisfied. However, the advantages of using a single tool can often outweigh the functionality of separate tools.

So what can be done? I think the first thing to remember is that every problem is at root a people problem (*Jerry Weinberg*). What that means for you and your JIRA is that decisions about using the tool need to be discussed and agreed upon by the people who use the tool. Tools can only help to reduce the barriers for people and groups working together; there is no magic tool to make people *want* to work together.

That said, this chapter describes some of the more common frustrations with JIRA and possible ways to avoid some of them. These include both things that annoy users if not configured properly by administrators, and aspects of JIRA that annoy JIRA administrators.

Add-Ons That Should Be Standard

There are some useful, well-supported, and even free (zero cost) add-ons that I install in almost every JIRA instance that I configure. This suggests to me that their functionality should be part of the core JIRA functionality. My four standard add-ons are currently:

JIRA Toolkit Plugin (http://bit.ly/12fYKfy)
> This is the grandfather of all JIRA add-ons, and contains too many useful features to list.

JIRA Suite Utilities (http://bit.ly/1boQaKN)
> Also known as JSU, this add-on has the custom fields, conditions, validators, and post functions that everyone uses.

JIRA Misc Workflow Extensions (http://bit.ly/ZFo2RE)
> JMWE has conditions, validators, and post-functions (the earlier name for "post functions"), all in a code base that has probably been used as the base for more customizations than any other add-on. JMWE become a commercial add-on in 2013 and is also available in JIRA Cloud.

ScriptRunner for JIRA (http://bit.ly/11uV3h1)
> ScriptRunner for JIRA, formerly Script Runner, lets you run scripts written in Groovy inside JIRA. Groovy is very similar to Java if you haven't used it before. The add-on also comes with customizable workflow conditions, validators and post functions, listeners, and services. No restarts are needed and there are no other add-ons to install. You get far greater flexibility for modifying JIRA and the ability to script many tedious administration tasks. It requires JIRA administrator permission to run such general scripts. Jamie Echlin, the author of this add-on, joined Adaptavist in 2015 and the plan is to make this a commercial add-on by the end of 2015.

Frustrations with Fields

One of the most common frustrations for users is having to enter data in fields that they don't understand or care about. This can happen in a number of ways:

- A field may be required by one team, but not another.

  The solution for this is to define a field configuration and screens for use by just that team's projects, along with the other schemes for their projects. Grouping projects into project categories can help with maintaining such schemes, as described in Chapter 4.

- The field's description may be missing or misleading.

  Don't accept a request for a new custom field unless it comes with a succinct and clear description of what the field is intended for. Then use that as the field's description. The description of a field in a field configuration overrides the original custom field description.

- The field's name is a duplicate.

  JIRA allows multiple custom fields with the same name, but it is almost always a mistake to do this because in some places you'll have multiple choices with no distinguishing information. If you do decide to do this, then at least give each field a good description.

- The field is being used as a combination of other fields.

  This can happen if custom fields aren't added when needed, so users overload an existing field (such as Summary) to record two or more pieces of information. For example, I've seen Summary fields that contain text such as "Showstopper: customer can't log in." The "Showstopper" part of that field should have been recorded in some other field, probably Priority, to allow better reporting later on. It's also easy to forget the convention, or use it without really understanding it (perhaps using it just because some other issues did).

- Required fields are not on the default tab.

  Just don't do this when you're designing screens. Put all the required fields on the default tab, so you don't forget that they're required during issue creation. Put them higher up on the screen so users don't have to scroll down to edit them.

Frustrations with Actions

Other frustrations for users center around issue actions and workflow transitions:

- Why can't I change an issue to a certain status?

  If it's just certain transitions, then it's probably due to conditions and validations that have been defined as part of the workflow for the issue. These conditions may or may not make any use of the Resolve Issues and Close Issues permissions, depending on how the workflow is configured (see Chapter 5).

  Adding the introduction gadget to the system dashboard and including links to documents that describe such expected restrictions can help. The ability to display the status of an issue within the workflow diagram can also help with this frustration.

- What permission do I need for a certain issue operation?

  The Permission Helper feature described in "Debugging Schemes" on page 26 can help administrators to debug these problems. Permissions are controlled with the permission scheme that an issue's project is using. To edit an issue, a user needs to have the Edit permission, which may be granted by project role or any of the other ways listed in the section "Adding Users to Schemes" on page 14.

Some of the less obvious permissions are noted in the section "Permission Schemes" on page 18. Changing a permission usually involves adding a user to a specific project role, rather than modifying the permission scheme.

- Why can't I bulk change some issues?

  The default JIRA workflow doesn't let you edit issues in the Closed status. So if you want to change a field in a hundred issues using Bulk Change but just one of those issues is closed, then JIRA won't let you change any of them. Sometimes there's an explanation given, but more often it's a puzzle to users and their administrators. Start with a smaller set of issues and see if you can bulk change those issues.

  Not all of an issue's fields can always be altered using a Bulk Change. For example, the Resolution field can only be changed if the field configuration hasn't hidden that field.

More Information Needed!

Sometimes users need more guidance about where to create or not create issues, and what should go into each field. What is needed is a way to add this information to JIRA's issue screens.

For just this reason, the *Message* custom field types are part of the standard *JIRA Tool kit add-on* available from Atlassian. These field types allow you to display text on an issue's screens. For example, the *Message Custom Field (for edit)* field type allows you to insert text between other fields on an edit screen. Other custom field types from the same add-on allow you to insert HTML to create the message. As shown in Figure 11-1, Atlassian uses these fields to provide additional guidance to users who are filing bugs with them.

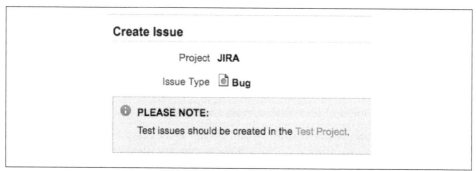

Figure 11-1. Adding helpful text to an issue screen

These message fields are defined just like any other custom field except that the text is set as a default value, and the fields are added to screens as usual. They don't have any values and do not appear in an issue otherwise. Sometimes they can appear unexpectedly on bulk change screens though. Since the message custom field names are not seen on the issue screens you can give them abstract names such as "Message 1" and "Message 2" and reuse them in multiple custom field contexts.

Frustrations with Email

How can you make sure that another user is notified of changes to a particular issue? That is what the Watchers system field is for. But even after another user has been added to the Watchers field, they won't receive email about the issue until the *next* change after that. It's like having a *Cc* on an email that only works for the next email.

Sometimes a user wants to just "poke" someone about an issue, but isn't sure who else will receive the email if they add a comment. This is like *Reply to All*, but without being able to see the *To* field. What is really needed is the current list of email recipients for each action, just for when it is wanted. The *JIRA Email This Issue Plugin* can help older versions of JIRA with this.

 Issues or lists of issues can be emailed to specific users with the Share link, along with an optional note. The @mention syntax allows you to add a comment and explicitly send an email to the @userid that was mentioned.

The Notification Helper feature described in "Debugging Schemes" on page 26 can help administrators debug why a particular user is not receiving email about changes to a certain issue.

Learning JIRA Safely

The first thing that any new administrator usually does with JIRA is to create a test project and a few test issues. The next thing they might do is change the default priorities and then start in on some workflow changes. A few minutes later, they wish they had made a backup and hadn't been playing around with the production JIRA instance.

Now, playing about is a *powerful way*[1] to learn any tool as a new user or administrator, but do it somewhere that won't matter when you make mistakes. Having a development or staging instance of JIRA is a great idea for this.

If you're concerned about sending email to other people as a result of your changes, then you can define an empty notification scheme for the JIRA project where you

---

1 "Let my playing be my learning, and my learning be my playing." — *Homo Ludens*, Johan Huizinga, 1938

are playing with issues. You could also do the same thing by just removing the notification scheme from a project, but using an empty scheme makes it clearer in Administration→Issues→Notification schemes as to which projects don't send email.

I also like to have a project named *SCRATCH* in production JIRA instances that is configured with the same schemes as one of my more heavily-used JIRA projects. I use that project to create test issues when checking my changes and avoid cluttering up any real projects.

Another thing I do is to maintain a separate JIRA project or component to track issues related to the local JIRA instance. This is using JIRA as a *meta-tracker* and it helps for all the same reasons you installed JIRA in the first place.

Too Many Administrators

Having too many JIRA administrators invariably leads to a JIRA instance with a confusing configuration. The temptation to experiment and hack until JIRA appears to do what you want seems to be irresistible. A main administrator, a couple of backup administrators, and maybe an IT-related administrator are usually all that should be needed. I recommend trimming the *jira-administrators* group regularly.

One oft-overlooked aspect of JIRA is that you can have both *jira-administrators* and *jira-system-administrators* groups. The differences between these two groups are described at *http://bit.ly/ZFou2b*. By default, the two groups are effectively the same, but one way to reduce what the existing JIRA administrators can do is to go to Administration→System→Global permissions, and set the group used for JIRA System Administrators to a new *jira-system-administrators* group.

You may wonder "Why have I got so many administrators in my JIRA?" The most likely explanation is that earlier versions of JIRA allowed only JIRA administrators to add components and versions to a project. This implied that project leads had to also be JIRA administrators, which often led to many users in the *jira-administrators* group. The better approach nowadays is to use JIRA project roles (see the section "Project Roles" on page 2), which let you grant project leads the permissions they need for their projects without destabilizing the rest of your JIRA instance. Adding new options to custom fields still needs JIRA administrative rights, but that kind of request can be better handled by filing a JIRA for the work with an administrator.

Better Feedback for Administrators

JIRA has always had a link to let users send email to the administrators of each JIRA instance. This can get confusing if there are many JIRA administrators, so there are two settings at Administration→System→Settings to customize the message seen by JIRA users wanting to contact an administrator.

Automating Your Configuration

A common task for a JIRA administrator is doing something that the UI makes easy for one and tedious for ten. For example, adding a user is easy, but adding ten users requires a lot of clicking. There are at least two ways to automate JIRA administration.

The first approach is to use the same *ScriptRunner* add-on by Jamie Echlin (Adaptavist) described in "Add-Ons That Should Be Standard" on page 111. This add-on has many canned scripts to do such things as copy the configuration from one project to another or modify resolutions in bulk. This add-on is also the most general way to access the underlying JIRA Java API for administration operations.

The second approach is to use a CLI as described in "CLI (Command Line Interface)" on page 100. The problem with this is that not all of the APIs you might want for administration are exposed by JIRA. This approach is relatively easy to use if you are only modifying issue or project data, but most administrative actions are harder (if even possible).

 I recommend using Adaptavist's ScriptRunner add-on for more complex JIRA administration. It comes with lots of built-in scripts but more complex use requires a little programming effort, and the documentation and support are excellent. Just remember to test the scripts on a staging JIRA instance, and to version control the scripts for later use.

JIRA used to support a deprecated scripting language named *Jelly*, but this was removed in JIRA 6.4.

For automating workflow actions (such as periodic escalation of issues or changing status when a comment is added), the *JIRA Automation Plugin* add-on by Atlassian (unsupported) is worth investigating.

Debugging Your Configuration

Working out why a user can't see or do something they expect can take a few frustrating minutes, even when you have a good procedure.

My approach, described in more detail in "Debugging Schemes" on page 26, is to note the issue's project and issue type, then go to the project's administration screen. Note the names of all of the schemes that the project is using and then view the appropriate one. For example, for permissions, view the named permission scheme and see which project roles are needed for the permission in question. Then return to the project's administration screen and go to the project's roles to see which users have that role in the project.

For more complex schemes (such as the issue type screen scheme), view the scheme and use the issue type to work out which screen scheme is being applied. Then look at that screen scheme to work out which of the screens is involved. Finally, view that screen to see whether the field is shown or not, and where.

Managing Custom Fields

Managing large numbers of custom fields (more than a few hundred) can be difficult because you have to scroll up and down to find the field you want. The "find" feature in your browser can help here. JIRA permits multiple custom fields with the same name and field type, so check carefully which issue types and projects each custom field is applied to. Even a single custom field can have multiple contexts, one per project, so you may have to click *Configure* for a field before you can see all the ways that a field is configured.

Managing Projects

JIRA 6.0 added the ability to edit a workflow scheme in place, which also updates the scheme for all other projects that are using it. Before this you had to manually update each project's workflow scheme if you added a new mapping from an issue type to a workflow, which could be very tedious if you had many projects, as noted at "The Hundred Tab Problem" (*JRA-25961*).

JIRA 6.0 also introduced the idea of project templates. When creating a new project you can choose from a number of predefined templates, which in turn use predefined schemes.

Once a JIRA project has been configured as intended, a common request is to create another project configured in exactly the same way. The new project will likely be part of a number of projects with the same category. JIRA has no built-in way to use a single project as a template for another, but the Project Creator for JIRA add-on (*https://marketplace.atlassian.com/plugins/com.wittified.jira.project-creator*) from Wittified can help with this.

Further Reading

There is an excellent presentation, "Seven Sins of Jira Administration" by Matthew Cobby (*http://www.slideshare.net/mcobby/seven-sins-of-jira-administration*) that contains a series of pithy patterns to avoid, plus characters familiar to all.

The JIRA Email This Issue Plugin can be found in the Atlassian marketplace (*https://marketplace.atlassian.com/plugins/com.metainf.jira.plugin.emailissue*).

Index

About the Author

Matt Doar is based in San Jose, CA where he works with ServiceRocket (formerly CustomWare), a professional services company that is also Atlassian's oldest and largest Expert. He has been helping other people with JIRA for over ten years and is the author of a number of JIRA add-ons and plugins as part of the wider Atlassian development community. He also wrote Practical JIRA Plugins (O'Reilly) and Practical Development Environments (O'Reilly), which described the basics of software tools—version control, build tools, testing, issue trackers, and automation. He has also held some sort of dubious record for the most bugs submitted about JIRA by a non-Atlassian. Before JIRA entered his world, Matt was a developer and then a software toolsmith at various networking companies. Before all that, he completed his B.A. and Ph.D. in Computer Networking at the University of Cambridge Computer Laboratory and St. John's College, Cambridge.

Colophon

The animals on the cover of *Practical JIRA Administration* are Cochin chickens (*Gallus domesticus*). There's been some discussion within Atlassian about which one is Mike and which one is Scott. This book is also known informally as the "Chicken Book."

The cover image is from the Dover Pictorial Archive. The cover font is Adobe ITC Garamond. The text font is Linotype Birka; the heading font is Adobe Myriad Condensed; and the code font is LucasFont's TheSans Mono Condensed.

Get even more for your money.

Join the O'Reilly Community, and register the O'Reilly books you own. It's free, and you'll get:

- $4.99 ebook upgrade offer
- 40% upgrade offer on O'Reilly print books
- Membership discounts on books and events
- Free lifetime updates to ebooks and videos
- Multiple ebook formats, DRM FREE
- Participation in the O'Reilly community
- Newsletters
- Account management
- 100% Satisfaction Guarantee

Signing up is easy:

1. Go to: oreilly.com/go/register
2. Create an O'Reilly login.
3. Provide your address.
4. Register your books.

Note: English-language books only

To order books online:
oreilly.com/store

For questions about products or an order:
orders@oreilly.com

To sign up to get topic-specific email announcements and/or news about upcoming books, conferences, special offers, and new technologies:
elists@oreilly.com

For technical questions about book content:
booktech@oreilly.com

To submit new book proposals to our editors:
proposals@oreilly.com

O'Reilly books are available in multiple DRM-free ebook formats. For more information:
oreilly.com/ebooks

O'REILLY®